Improvised Projections

DISTANZ

Improvised Projections

Philipp Goldbach
with Steffen Siegel

KONTEXT

Contents

Improvised Projections
Foreword

These days, we have gotten used to being able to find every conceivable image online with just a few clicks, and our digital devices allow us to use them for any number of purposes: for research, presentation, or simply contemplation. But how did people access images in the pre-digital age—or at least before digital technology commandeered every area of work and life? And which strategies did they use in countries where state censorship restricted access to undesirable material or even made it a criminal offense? This was the case in the German Democratic Republic, where literature published in the Federal Republic of Germany—so-called *Westliteratur* (West literature)—was subject to especially strict state controls that almost completely prevented its distribution. Alongside dangerous acts of outright defiance, people also developed innovative detours that tread a more inconspicuous path—ways of acquiring knowledge that operated in gray areas unlikely to attract criminal prosecution.

Andreas Krase, the first historian of photography at the renowned Hochschule für Grafik und Buchkunst (HGB, Academy of Visual Arts) in Leipzig, trod one such path when he started teaching there in 1985. He took advantage of the fact that Leipzig—like Frankfurt am Main after World War II—was home to the Deutsche Nationalbibliothek (then known as the Deutsche Bücherei), where every book published in Germany had to be catalogued. Even though there was a special program known as the *Giftschrank* (poison cabinet) for storing ideologically suspect works, the collection of viewable art books was still extensive, especially those on photography. Krase began compiling his own teaching materials on slide film using a self-made reproduction device. Over the years, he built up a remarkable collection of reproductions from the beginnings of photography with Joseph Nicéphore Niépce through modernism with August Sander to Diane Arbus in the nineteen-seventies. Krase produced around 3,200 reproductions at the Deutsche Bücherei, the Staatsbibliothek zu Berlin, and the university's own library, among other places, which, when added to the HGB's prior collection, brought the total to nearly 4,000.

The 35mm slide format became especially popular after the war as it combined brilliant color reproduction and high resolution with easy handling. It was thus widely used in commercial photography but also became common in private settings, such as giving travel reports at social gatherings. Its advantages for teaching almost go without saying. The slide magazine could be loaded with images on a specific topic which were then "cast onto the wall" in any size—but unlike photographically illustrated books, or "imaginary museums" as André Malraux put it, they had the advantage of being viewable by many students at the same time. Krase not only developed and framed most of his photographs himself, but also carefully catalogued them in a register, where they were consecutively numbered and captioned with information about the images, their sources, and, in most cases, the locations of the publications.

The end of the GDR marked a period of political upheaval, which—coincidentally—was soon followed by the end of photography's analog age. It left behind a multitude of objects, materialized symbols of a particular era, most of which could now be considered historical. The relics considered culturally valuable have been and continue to be preserved and cared for, with the especially valuable ones being integrated into archives, while the simpler everyday items are sometimes sold off at flea markets, kept for personal reasons, and passed on to heirs—or sorted out and irretrievably destroyed.

Nowadays, university lecture halls and seminar rooms are usually equipped with digital projectors, while their slide collections have either already been disposed of or otherwise disappeared into the institutions' basement storage. Since 2013, the artist Philipp Goldbach has focused on transforming these slide libraries into works of art: densely stacked to form digital-looking wall reliefs; repurposed as a usable dance floor where the slides are lit up with colored lights to musical rhythms; or chaotically scattered on the floor of the exhibition space. Hundreds of thousands of slides thus become preserved in Goldbach's installations, although they are no longer projected as individual images.

These former objects of collective knowledge generation are transformed into works of art whose formal designs and performative aspects open up new and unique perspectives on the medium and the decades-old storage systems associated with it. For Andreas Krase's slide library, he collaborated with photo theorist Steffen Siegel to develop a wall installation that supplements Krase's slide archive with a four-part display using inlays of original slide cabinets from VEB Foto und Feinmesstechnik Mulda (see pp. 150/151) and a small dictionary on the history of photography in the GDR written by Siegel. Their joint work is titled *Lossless Compression (Diathek Fotografiegeschichte Andreas Krase)*.

In this book, Goldbach's "lossless compression" and Siegel's photo-historical keywords are accompanied by Krase's complete index, which lists, line by line, those images that are deliberately rendered invisible in Goldbach's artistic version. These are captions to 150 years of photography history, which readers can wander through on more than ninety pages, with each line opening up a new image. These "prompts" appeal to our visual memory, to our imaginary museums, while the contexts they are embedded in recall the fact that education and knowledge transfer are not simply a matter of course, and must sometimes be secured by improvised means.

Analog

Andreas Krase created his slide library in the mid-nineteen-eighties, at a time when the coming media revolution was already looming on the horizon. Shortly thereafter, around 1995, photography would become a digital affair. This transition not only affected the practices of photographic production, but also the way such images were used. In seminars that employed visual materials, the hum of the projector came to replace the characteristic clacking of a slide carousel advancing. To this day, large image collections of disused slides continue to be stored in the basements of many institutions.

Jens Schröter, Alexander Böhnke (eds.), *Analog/Digital – Opposition oder Kontinuum? Zur Theorie und Geschichte einer Unterscheidung* (Bielefeld: Transcript, 2004).

Beiler, Berthold (1915–1975)

was, according to one of his book covers, "the leading Marxist-Leninist theorist of photography in the GDR—closely associated with the practical development of the photographers' movement in socialism." In 1967, the Fotokinoverlag Leipzig published his magnum opus *Die Gewalt des Augenblicks. Gedanken zur Ästhetik der Fotografie* (The Power of the Moment: Thoughts on the Aesthetics of Photography). He was deputy chairman of the *Zentrale Kommission Fotografie* in the Kulturbund der DDR (Cultural Association of the GDR), but from 1960 onwards he mainly taught aesthetics and theory of photography at the Hochschule für Grafik und Buchkunst (HGB, Academy of Visual Arts) in Leipzig. Beiler's interest in photography was systematic in nature, though his work did not focus on any specific aspect of the history of photography.

Berthold Beiler, *Parteilichkeit im Foto* (Halle/Saale: Fotokinoverlag, 1959); *Die Gewalt des Augenblicks. Gedanken zur Ästhetik der Fotografie*, 2nd expanded edition (Leipzig: Fotokinoverlag, 1969 [1967]); *Weltanschauung der Fotografie: Beiträge zu einer marxistischen Ästhetik der Fotografie* (Leipzig: Fotokinoverlag, 1977); *Denken über Fotografie* (Leipzig: Fotokinoverlag, 1977).

Black and White

Only a rather small part of photographic history is actually in black and white. Before the invention of color photography, photographs were brown, yellow, blue, or silver—they could take on a remarkable spectrum of different tonalities. When we speak about the history of black-and-white photographs, what we are dealing with is usually the reproduction of such images. For a long time, they had to be reduced to grayscale to be reproduced in books or magazines, as this helped keep the production costs in manageable limits. Andreas Krase's slide library is no exception. Producing thousands of images on color film would have increased the total cost many times over. Then there was another factor that was just as important: in the makeshift lab in his apartment, Andreas Krase could only develop black-and-white film. Pragmatism and improvisation were not only essential to the production of the slide library, but also how it was used. As in art history classes, the collective viewing of the images took place within a framework dictated by the reproduction technology. The rich spectrum of colors had to be left to the viewer's imagination.

Monika Wagner, Helmut Lethen (eds.), *Schwarz-Weiß als Evidenz* (Frankfurt am Main, New York: Campus, 2015).

Canon

Andreas Krase's slide library consists of around 4,000 slides. The lecturer produced more than three quarters of it himself. Over a period of roughly four years, he had to make several thousand decisions about which photographs—mostly printed images—to select, reproduce, and integrate into his teaching collection. He thus created an essential tool for teaching the history of photography. Krase was particularly interested in the first hundred years, from the eighteen to nineteen-twenties. Each individual decision in favor of a particular image resulted in a collection that reveals a personal view of photographic history: Krase's interest in certain things, his personal affinity for certain stories that he wanted to unpack in the seminar room. The result was a canon of the history of photography in the original sense of the word: a measure, a guideline. It allowed students to learn to see the diversity of possible photographic histories.

Lee Morrissey (ed.), *Debating the Canon: A Reader from Addison to Nafisi* (New York: Palgrave Macmillan, 2005).

Chance

The slide library's coherence can give an impression of completeness. In fact, it was the product of years of persistent research by Andreas Krase. At the same time, it was also shaped by external conditions far beyond the lecturer's control. His canon of the history of photography was only able to integrate sources available to him at the Deutsche Bücherei and other collections in East Germany. Often enough, the restrictions that applied to all information acquisition in the GDR—and ultimately chance—played a major part in determining this slide library.

Deutsche Bücherei

Since its founding in 1912, the Deutsche Bücherei in Leipzig has collected all printed matter published in German and made it available to the public. This practice also continued under a divided Germany. As a result, publications from West German publishers could also be consulted in the Leipzig reading rooms—something that was rarely possible elsewhere in the GDR. This made the "DB," as it is users often still call it, into a privileged place of reading—even if there were considerable hurdles to accessing it. Not everyone could simply order anything from the holdings, especially when it came to political writings. However, literature on the history of photography was generally unaffected by such regulations. It remained available for attentive reading and viewing, especially for a knowledgeable image collector like Andreas Krase.

Christian Rau, *"Nationalbibliothek" im geteilten Land. Die Deutsche Bücherei 1945–1990* (Göttingen: Wallstein, 2018).

Fotokinoverlag

was the first stop for anyone in the GDR who wanted to learn more about photography. Its predecessor, Wilhelm Knapp Verlag, founded in Halle in 1838, was already one of the most important publishers of specialist literature on photography. In 1957, it was converted into a state-owned enterprise (VEB) and given its new name, which it retained until its dissolution in 1991. From 1964 onwards, it was an imprint of Fachbuchverlag Leipzig. In its three and a half decades of operation, Fotokinoverlag published more than 700 books. In addition to specialist publications and popular guides to photographic practice, it also released elaborately printed illustrated books on the history and present of photography. Last but not least, it was also known for two monthly magazines: *Fotografie* (1947–1991) and *Fotokino-Magazin* (1962–1991).

Christoph Links, *Das Schicksal der DDR-Verlage. Die Privatisierung und ihre Konsequenzen* (Berlin: Ch. Links, 2009), pp. 74–75.

History of Photography

One of the peculiar things about photography is that people have been interested in its history ever since the technique was developed. Even the earliest writings on photography regularly mention its origins and evolution. But it would take more than a century before the study of the medium's history became a serious academic subject. In the nineteen-seventies, this topic eventually found its way into university curricula, first in the US and shortly thereafter in Europe. The courses offered by Andreas Krase at the Hochschule für Grafik und Buchkunst (HGB, Academy of Visual Arts) in Leipzig since the mid-eighties were among the earliest ones on the history of photography to be regularly held at a German university.

Maren Gröning (ed.), *Frame and Focus: Photography as a Schooling Issue* (Salzburg: Fotohof Edition, 2015).

Hochschule für Grafik und Buchkunst (Academy of Visual Arts) Leipzig

Founded in 1764, it is among the oldest art academies in Germany. In the GDR, it was one of the most important training centers for the visual arts; and for photography, it was simply the most important. After the Fachschule für angewandte Kunst in Magdeburg was closed in 1963, photographic training at university level was concentrated in Leipzig. The professors and lecturers included Heinz Föppel, Sieghard Liebe, Klaus Liebich, Wolfgang G. Schröter, Helfried Strauß, and Horst Thorau. Arno Fischer, however, was certainly the most renowned. In addition, Evelyn Richter taught as a lecturer in Leipzig from 1980 onwards and, like Fischer, she shaped an entire generation of photographers.

Arno Rink (ed.), *Hochschule für Grafik und Buchkunst Leipzig 1945–1989. Eine Ausstellung der Hochschule für Grafik und Buchkunst Leipzig und des Museums der bildenden Künste Leipzig anläßlich des 225. Jubiläums der Hochschule* (Leipzig: Seemann, 1989).

Home-made

Often enough, the art of improvisation led to "home-made" devices. In Andreas Krase's case, it was a mobile device for photographically reproducing images. Klaus Liebich, a lecturer at the Hochschule für Grafik und Buchkunst (HGB, Academy of Visual Arts), helped tailor it specifically to the photo historian's needs: a portable device with a flash that could be attached to the camera itself and took up very little space when dismantled. It enabled Krase to produce high-quality photographic copies regardless of the light conditions at the respective venues. Most of the time, he worked in a study separate from the Deutsche Bücherei's main reading rooms.

Zeitschrift für Medienwissenschaft, no. 27 (September 2022), "Reparaturwissen: DDR," ed. by Ulrike Hanstein, Manuela Klaut, and Jana Mangold.

Images

The development of the history of photography is best studied through images. Though this wasn't always the case. Until well into the twentieth century, the reproduction of images in print was a laborious and costly affair. This becomes evident when leafing through early books on the history of photography. For example, the 4th edition of Josef Maria Eder's standard work *Ausführliches Handbuch der Photographie* from 1932 recounts the medium's history on more than 1,110 pages—but Eder unfolds this history almost entirely without illustrations. Instead, the focus lies on technical apparatuses and processes. Essentially, it was a technological history of photography. Only with the advent of significantly simpler and cheaper printing processes did it become possible to illustrate books comprehensively. These advances opened up a new perspective that has had a lasting impact on our understanding of the history of images, not least that of photography.

Steffen Siegel, *Fotogeschichte aus dem Geist des Fotobuchs* (Göttingen: Wallstein, 2019).

Improvisation

Etymologically, the word "improvisation" refers to the unpredictable. One thing, however was always certain in the GDR: improvisation would be necessary. In the East German state, it was a cultural technique required in many spheres of life, not least in acquiring information. Andreas Krase's photographic slide archive is but one important example. At the time, the infrastructure that the Hochschule für Grafik und Buchkunst (HGB, Academy of Visual Arts) provided for viewing the history of photography was sparse at best. Apart from a few volumes in the university library, any images that lecturers wanted to discuss with their students would first have to be researched, collected, reproduced, and stored. It required a talent for improvisation, and in Krase's case it meant creating his own reproduction device to be used in the Deutsche Bücherei.

Information Acquisition

With respect to the GDR, historian Jürgen Kocka aptly spoke of a thoroughly "dominated society"—a diagnosis that we can also apply to the way information had to be acquired. There was nothing like a free circulation of knowledge. Gaining access to knowledge remained a matter of individual tenacity, skill, and, not least, the art of improvisation. Anyone who, like Andreas Krase, was involved in designing a new field of study was well advised to spend time in academic libraries such as the Deutsche Bücherei in Leipzig. It was the only place where it was possible to research the full spectrum of historical and contemporary literature on photography—including the better-printed books from West German publishers.

Krase, Andreas (b. 1958)

studied art history at Humboldt Universität in Berlin after training as a photographic technician. From 1985 to 1990, he worked as a research assistant at the Hochschule für Grafik und Buchkunst (HGB, Academy of Visual Arts) in Leipzig, then held other teaching positions there until 1992. Krase regularly taught seminars on the history of photography, and he was the first person at any German university to consistently focus on this academic field. Later on, he received his doctorate from Humboldt Universität with a thesis on the metal sculptor and photographer Fritz Kühn. From 1993 to 1998, Krase worked at the Berlinische Galerie, and from 1999 to 2004 he was responsible for the supervision of the Hermann Krone Collection at the Technische Universität Dresden. He then went on to become the curator of photography at the Technischen Sammlungen Dresden, where he remained until his retirement in 2024.

Andreas Krase, Fritz Kühn, *Das photographische Werk 1931–1967* (Berlin: Nicolai Verlag, 1998); *Dresden in Photographien des 19. Jahrhunderts* (Munich: Schirmer Mosel, 2020).

ORWO

Since 1964, it has been the company name of the only manufacturer of film material in the GDR. The four letters are an abbreviation for "Original Wolfen," and the company emerged from the Agfa corporation. ORWO was one of the most important companies in the GDR's so-called chemical triangle, which stretched between Halle, Merseburg, and Bitterfeld—a region that suffered dramatic environmental pollution at the time.

Silke Fengler, *Entwickelt und fixiert. Zur Unternehmens- und Technikgeschichte der deutschen Fotoindustrie, dargestellt am Beispiel der Agfa AG Leverkusen und des VEB Filmfabrik Wolfen (1945–1995)* (Essen: Klartext Verlag, 2009).

Pachnicke, Peter (1942–2019)

studied philosophy and art history in Berlin and succeeded Berthold Beiler as professor of aesthetics at the Hochschule für Grafik und Buchkunst (HGB, Academy of Visual Arts) in Leipzig. Andreas Krase's seminars on the history of photography filled a gap in Beiler's and Pachnicke's course offerings. Pachnicke also worked as a curator for national and international art exhibitions. After the end of the GDR, he was forced to give up his professorship and became a curator at the Ludwiggalerie in Schloss Oberhausen.

Peter Pachnicke (ed.), *Alltag und Epoche. Werke bildender Kunst der DDR aus 35 Jahren* (Berlin: Henschelverlag Kunst u. Gesellschaft, 1984; licensed edition West Berlin: Elefanten Press, 1984).

Photocopiers

For a long time, these devices were one of the most important tools for acquiring information, especially in libraries. As a matter of fact, photocopiers were also manufactured in the GDR: there was the "Pentacop" by the Dresden-based company Pentacon, which was best known for its Praktica cameras, and the "Secop" by VEB Secura-Werke in Berlin. In the GDR, however, their use was strictly regulated. The reproduction of documents was closely monitored—the political motivations for such restrictions in an unfree society are easy to imagine. Such devices, when available at all, could only be used in public institutions like the Deutsche Bücherei, and only with high fees. A single photocopy cost 20 pfennig. Given the relatively low salaries paid in the GDR, such an amount was almost prohibitive. But it is also important to note that there was a completely different photocopier in use: the camera. It was the preferred tool for a special form of improvisation. Despite the high prices for 35mm film and the associated effort, entire books were reproduced in this way.

Photographie – Fotografie

This was the title of an exhibition known in full as *Photographie – Fotografie. 150 Jahre Bild und Technik aus Sammlungen und Archiven der DDR*. It was presented from February 10 through April 2, 1989 at the Ephraim Palace in Berlin, the capital of the GDR. The timing of the exhibition was hardly incidental: in 1839, several photographic processes were presented to the public more or less simultaneously—one could speak, with some exaggeration, of photography's "year of birth." *Medium Fotografie*, an exhibition which took place in 1977 in Halle/Saale, had already attempted a cultural-historical overview of photography, and the accompanying catalog was also licensed for distribution in the Federal Republic of Germany. Twelve years later, *Photographie – Fotografie* brought together a dozen curators, including Andreas Krase, who shared the idea of exploring the wealth of photographic collections in very different locations throughout the GDR. It was the first exhibition to bring these collections together in a single place. At the same time, the exhibition was the result of a remarkable form of cooperation, jointly sponsored by VEB Carl Zeiss Jena and the Gesellschaft für Fotografie of the Kulturbund der DDR. Unfortunately, this exhibition was not accompanied by a catalog.

Andreas Hüneke, Gerhard Ihrke, Alfred Neumann, Ullrich Wallenburg (eds.), *Medium Fotografie* (Leipzig: Fotokinoverlag, 1979; licensed edition West Berlin: Elefanten Press, 1981).

Praktica

This was the brand name for a series of single-lens reflex cameras manufactured by VEB Pentacon Dresden. The history of this camera dates back to the years before the GDR. Incidentally, the brand name is often misspelled (Practica, Praktika, Practika). The correct spelling is with a "k" at the beginning and a "c" at the end. However, Andreas Krase did not use a camera produced in the GDR for his reproductions, but a Nikon FM, which delivered significantly higher quality images than the standard Praktica cameras. It was thus Japanese technology that enabled the creation of an image archive on the history of photography in Leipzig.

Roger Rössing, *Fotografie mit der Praktica,* 15th revised edition (Halle/Saale: Fotokinoverlag, 1986 [1959]); *Richard Hummel, Spiegelreflexkameras aus Dresden. Geschichte – Technik – Fakten* (Leipzig: Edition Reintzsch, 1995).

Register

The labor invested by Andreas Krase was not limited to just producing the slides, but also managing them. His most important tool for this was a typewritten register. It listed all slides chronologically according to their production. Each entry starts with a number and contains a caption with additional information about the photographer, the subject of the image, the date of the original, and a reference to the source Krase used. In most cases, these were books that he systematically skimmed for this purpose. The register's very first entry may be surprising to some, as the motif is somewhat unusual when it comes to the history of photography: a view of Chichen Itza in Mexico, dated around 1860, by the French archaeologist and photographer Désiré Charnay.

Umberto Eco, *The Infinity of Lists* (New York: Rizzoli, 2009).

Reproduction

The history of photography began with the desire to reproduce not only the visible world, but also preexisting images. One of the most important pioneers of photography, the Frenchman Nicéphore Niépce, experimented with ways of reproducing copperplate engravings and etchings. At its core, photography is thus not only a reproductive process for mirroring realities. Such images created with the aid of an apparatus can always be related to other, already existing images. Anyone who, like Andreas Krase, sought to create an image archive on the history of photography comprising thousands of photographs thus found themselves working on an archive of reproduced reproductions.

Heinz Hamann, *Fotografische Reproduktion* (Leipzig: Fotokinoverlag, 1990).

Research Assistant

Much like everywhere else, university careers in the GDR were pursued in stages. The position of a research assistant was often the first step in climbing the university ladder. Andreas Krase was hired as such at the Hochschule für Grafik und Buchkunst (HGB, Academy of Visual Arts) in 1985, albeit under peculiar circumstances. Since the staffing plan did not provide for the position of a lecturer in the history of photography, the vacant position of assistant to professor Werner Tübke was reassigned after internal discussions. The fact that this famous painter's work primarily engaged with the Old Masters may or may not have overlapped with Krase's interests. Ultimately, they never met in person. At the time, Tübke was preoccupied with something else entirely: completing the huge panorama in Bad Frankenhausen about the German Peasants' War, which was finally unveiled in the fall of 1989. Krase's time at the university came to an end in 1992.

Slides

The earliest versions of image projection techniques date back far beyond the history of photography, and projection quickly came to play an important role in the medium's development. Art historical education, in particular, has benefited enormously from it. A "picture cast onto a wall" invites a large audience to simultaneously view the image as a group. What we take for granted today was only introduced to lecture halls shortly before 1900, and it soon became clear that a second projector would be necessary for accurate analysis, since two images projected next to each other allow for direct comparison. Krase's slide archive is directly connected to this established practice but adds something of its own. In his work, it is photography itself—not painting, sculpture, or graphic art—that became the exclusive subject of photographic reproduction.

Tal-Or Ben-Choreen and Karla McManus, "The Slide Lecture," *History of Photography*, vol. 47, no. 1 (2023). Anne Lacoste et al. (eds.), *Slides. The History of Projected Photography* (Lausanne: Editions Noir sur Blanc, 2017). Jens Ruchatz, *Licht und Wahrheit. Eine Mediumgeschichte der fotografischen Projektion* (Munich: Wilhelm Fink, 2003).

VEB Foto Kino Mulda

Founded in 1898 under the name Berlebach, the company is based in Mulda, Saxony. Nationalized in 1972, it was the GDR's most important supplier of camera accessories, especially wooden tripods which were distinguished by having particularly low vibration. The company also manufactured small cabinets for storing slide positives out of lightweight wood. Each cabinet held 250 slides. A numbering system inside kept everything organized and, in combination with a typewritten index, allowed users to easily access the image archive. Andreas Krase ended up needing a total of eight of these cabinets for the 4,000 images he used in his teaching over the years.

John Tagg, "The Archiving Machine; or, The Camera and the Filing Cabinet," *Grey Room*, no. 47 (Spring 2012), pp. 24–37.

Work

Andreas Krase's image archive comprises almost 4,000 slides. He made most of them using analog photographic material from the company ORWO. In total, it amounts to more than a hundred 35mm film rolls, each with 36 individual images. A whole chain of practices precedes each frame: from researching and selecting the motif, preparing the shot (often in the Deutsche Bücherei in Leipzig), to taking the picture itself, developing the film, and cropping the individual images, which then had to be framed, glued, and labeled. Finally, Krase recorded all images in a register using a typewriter, before sorting them into slide cabinets manufactured by VEB Foto Kino Mulda. Is it possible to say how much time he spent on each image in this process? If we make a conservative estimate of only fifteen minutes per image, it would amount to about 1,000 hours or almost 42 days of non-stop work.

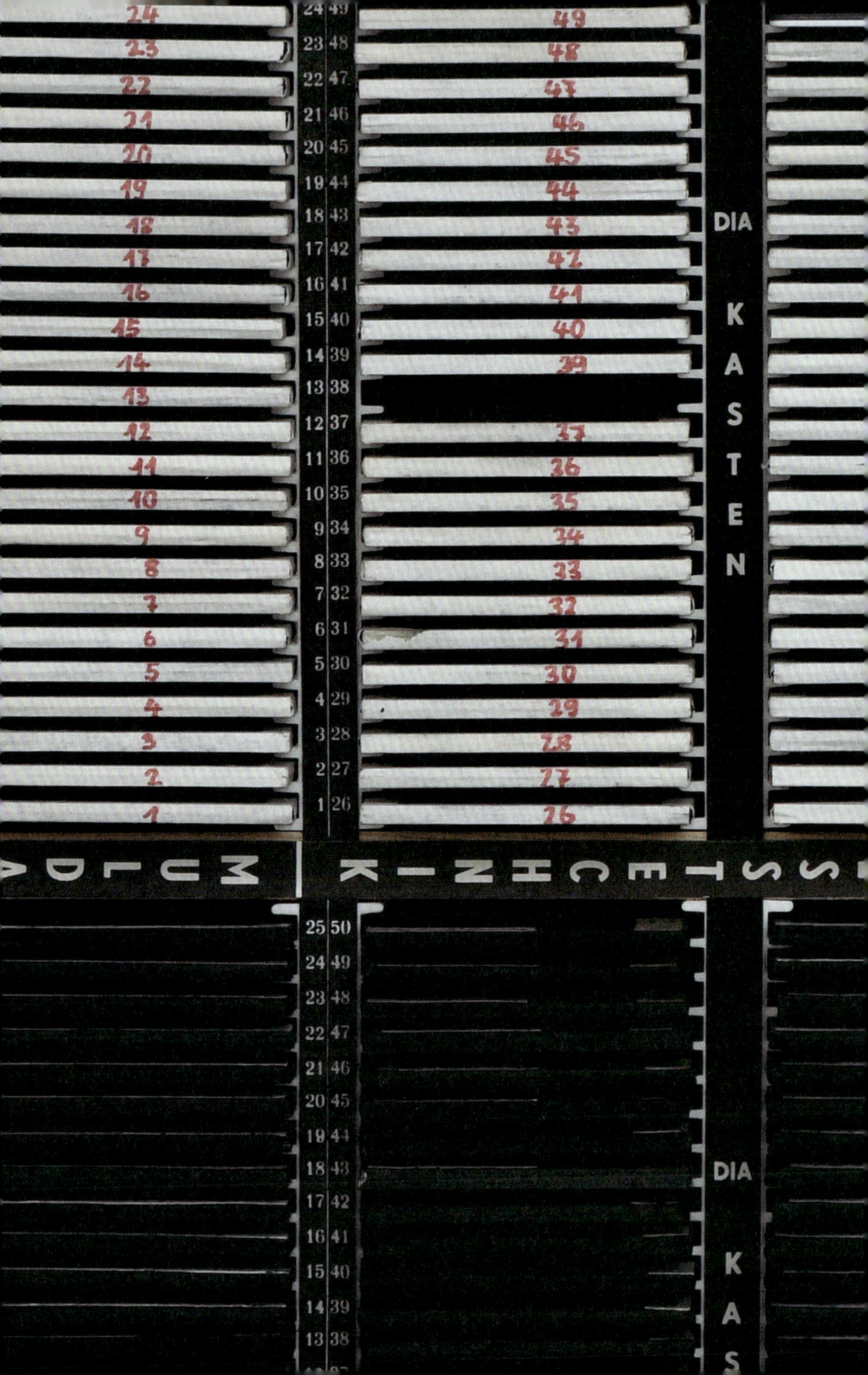

Bruce Bernard, The Sunday Times book of Photodiscovery. 1
A Century of Extraordinary Images 1840 - 1940, London 1980

1 Désiré Charnay, Fr. , Chichen - Itza, Mexico, ca 1860 Ap

2 Samuel Bourne GB, Das Cawnpore Memorial, ca 1865 Ap

3 Adolphe Braun, Fr., Stilleben mit Reh und Wildgans, ca 1865, Karbondruck

4 Collard, Fr., Rundgebäude der Bourbonnais - Eisenbahn, Nevers, 1862-67 Ap

5 Felice A. Beato, GB, Hypostyle /Säulenhalle in Edfu, nach 1862 Ap

6 Camille Silvy, Fr., Straßen-Musiker in Porchester Terrace, London, ca 1860 Ap

7 An., Niagara-Fälle mit Turm, ca 1860 Ap

8 An.,GB, Ein ausgedienter Veteran und seine Frau, ca 1860 Ambrotype, handkoloriert

9 William Notman (Can,) Victoria-Brücke über den Lawrence,Ap, Stereo 1858

10 An, Verlegung des Atlantikkabels (?) 1858, Ap, Stereo

11 Comte Olympe Aguado, Fr., Bewunderung , 1860 Ap

12, Charles Piazzi Smyth, Schottland, Unwissende Zuschauer, Nowgorod, 1859 Ambrotype, handkol.

13 Roger Fenton, Odalisque, 1858 SAlzpapier

14 Captain Linnaeus Tripe GB, Tempelfestung in Südindien, Ap vor 1858 Wachspapierneg.

15 Nadar, Selbstporträt mit Mme Nadar und Paul Nadar ca 1865 Ap

16 An, verm. USA, Akt-Modell, o.D. Ap

17 Atelier Held (Schweiz), Bauleute, ca 1890 Ap

18 Jules Robuchon, Fr., Saint Jouin- des-Marnes, Ruinen des Klosters, ca 1885 Woodburytype

19 Etienne Carjat, Léon Gambetta auf seinem Totenbett, 1882 Kohledruck

20 An (GB, Asyl Patient von Melancholie befallen, 1876 Ap

21 W.L. Skeen & Co, GB, Tamilen-Mädchen, ca 1880, Ap

22 An, verm.GB, Siamesischer Junge, Musiker, ca 1875 Ap

23 John Thomson, Die Brücke in Foo Chow, 1873, von Foo Chow und dem Fluß Min, Kohledruck

24 Fred Hardie (verm. USA), Berber, Unterhaltungskünstler, Tanger, 1870er Ap

25 Dr. A. de Montmeja (Fr.), Linearer Einschnitt des Auges veröffentlicht 1875 retusch Ap

26 Mac Pherson, Die Fälle von Terni, vor 1867 Ap

27 An, Taucher am Pier N° 4, Kansas City-Brücke, 1868 Ap
28 Charles Marville, Das Pantheon während der Rekonstruktion, ca 1870 Ap
29 J. Andrieu, Die Brücke in Argentieul, 1870/71 Ap
30 Mac Pherson, Bas-Relief im Innern des Titusgrabes, Rom, ca 1865 Ap
31 Paul Nadar, Michel Chevreul, 1886 Ap
32 Julia Margaret Cameron, Mary Hillier, ca 1867 Ap

David Plowden, Landscape, Introduction by Ian Jeffrey, Tokyo 1984
La Photographie d'Art, Douglas Davis, Paris 1984

33 Talbot, Hüte, 1844 Kalot.
34 Hill und Adamson, Seeleute in Newhaven 1843-45, Steinmetze bei der Arbeit am Scott-Denkmal, da 1845 Kalot.
35 Hill und Adamson , John Stevens naben einer römischen Büste, 1843-45, Kalot.
36 Hill und Adamson, Wohnhaus in Newhaven, 1845, Kalot.
37 Hill und Adamson, Fischerfrauen in Newhaven, ca 1845 "
38 D.O. Hill, Detail des Gemäldes mit der Darstellung der Gründung der Schottischen Freikirche, Mei 1843
39 Talbot, Haus gegenüber dem Hotel, wo T im Mai 1843 wohnte, Paris Kalot.
40 Talbot, Talbots Töchter im Garten, 1842 Kalot.
41 Talbot, Mikrophotographien mit Hilfe eines Sonnenmikroskops aufgenommen, 1839 - 41 Kalot.
42 Talbot, Die offene Tür, Pencil of Nature, 1843 Kaloty.
43 Talbot, Der Kreuzgang von Lacock Abbey mit Reverent Calvert Jones, ca 1843 Kalot.
44 Johann Baptist Isenring, Porträt von Carl Baumgartner, ca 1847, Kal., A. Löcherer, Schachspieler, Kalot.
45 Maxime Du Camp, Ägypt. Relief,1852 Kalot.,Koloss Ramses II in Abu Simbel, 1849-51, Kalot.
46 Humbert de Molard, Jäger, 1851 Kalot.
47 Comte Olympe Aguado, Stilleben, ca 1850 Kalot.
48 Eugène Durieu, Halbakt in einer Pose von Eugène Delacroix ca 1854 Koll.
49 E. Baldus, Befestigungen in Avignon, 1851 Kalot.
50 Auguste Salzmann, Jüd. Sarkophag in Jerusalem, 1854 Jerusalem, 1855-56, Kalot.
51 Charles Nègre, Orgelspieler, 1851 Kalot.
52 Julien Vallou de Villeneuve, Akt ca 1854, Wachspapier

53 Francis Frith, Die große Pyramide von Gizeh, 1859 Ap
54 Frith, Der Koloss Ramses II von Abu Simbel, Nubien
ca 1862 Ap
55 Charles Nègre, Drehorgelspieler, 1853 Papierneg. Ap
56 Gustave le Gray, Am Ende des Gartens, 1853 Ap
57 Le Gray, Französisches Militärmanöver auf den Feldern
von Chalons, 1857 kol. Ap
58 Adolphe Braun, Blumenstück, 1857 Ap
59 Der Amateur von Cromer, Blumenstilleben, 1845 Dag.
60 Carleton E. Watkins, Washingtonsäule, Yosemite, Californien, 1866 Ap
61 Herrmann Vogel, Brücke nahe dem Königsgrab, Ap
62 An. (Engl.) Mrs William Morris, 1865 Ap
63 Oscar G. Rejlander, Schwere Zeiten, 1869, Ap
64 William Lake Price, Don Quichote in seinem Arbeitszimmer, 1857 Ap
65 Der Amateur von Cromer, Stilleben, gegen 1845 Dag.
66 Nadar, Gustav Doré, 1854 Salzpapier
67 Julia M. Cameron, Alice Liddell als Pomona, 1872 Ap
68 D.O. Hill und Alexander McGlasthan, Am Weinspalier,
1862 Ap
69 Hill und Adamson, Miss. Chalmers und ihr Sohn, 1844-48, Kalot.
70 Alfred Stieglitz, Die Netzflickerin, 1894 Platindr.
71 Gertrude Käsebier, Frauenporträt ca 1900 Gummibichromat
72 Alvin Langdon Coburn, Das Schiff, Docks von Liverppol,
ca 1906. Platindr.
73 Robert Demachy, Die Menge, 1910 Pigmentdr.
74 Clarence H. White, Der Kuß, 1904 Platindr.
75 R. Demachy, Ballerinen, 1897 Gummidr.
76 R. Demachy, Studie in Rot, 1898 Gummidr.
77 Edward Steichen, Der Tag des Hindernisrennens, Paris 1911 Gel-karbondr.
78 Thomas Eakins, Mary Macdowell, 188 o Platindr.
79 Baron von Stillfried, Japanische Gläubige, 1870-80 kol. Ap

David Plowden, Landscape, Tokyo 1984

80 Peter Henry Emerson, Heimkehr von der Flußmündung, Norfolk, 1886 Platindr.
81 George Baker, Niagara Fälle, 1888 Ap
82 Henry Peach Robinson, Seemöven, o.D. Ap
83 An. (Fr.) Jean Baptist Corot, ca 1870 Ap
84 Robert Mc Pherson, Neptungrotte, Italien, 1862 Ap
85 Louis Alphonse de Brébisson, Studie von im Wasser reflektierten Bäumen, 1855 Ap
86 Humbert de Molard, Normannische Hütte mit Figur, 1847 - 50 Salzpapier
87 An.(GB)Ländl. Wohnkate, Silbergelatineprint, Calot.neg. ca 1850

88 Daguerre, Komposition mit Muscheln, Dag., 1837

Julia van Haaften, From Talbot to Stieglitz, London 1982

89 Mathew B. Brady, Kommittee der Schönen Künste der New Yorker Metropolitan Ausstellung 1864
90 whrsch. Felice Antonio Beato, Prinz Okudaira, ca 1867
91 Edward Sherriff Curtis, Canon del Muerte, ca 1900
92 whrsch. Felice A. Beato, Frau in Winterkleidung, ca 1867
93 Edward Muybrigde, Laufendes Kind, ca 1884-87
94 - " -- , Fliegender Kakadou, 1884-87

Werner Hofmann, Panorama einer Vergangenheit. Die ersten dreißig Jahre, Buchmuseum DB Leipzig

95 Talbot, Schloß Abbotsford, Sun Pictures in Scotland, 1844
96 Talbot, o.T. (Einfahrt)zum Schloß) ca 1845
97 Eynard-Lullin (; 1775-1863) Gent, E.-L. und Frau, ca 1842 Dag.
98 An., Wien, Akt, Stereodagerreotypie, ca 1853
99 Southworth /Hawes, General Wool, ca 1850 Dag.

1oo Felice A. Beato, Japanische Landarbeiter, 1867/68 kol. Ap
1o1 Adam Clark Vroman, Eichen auf der Baldwin-Ranch, 19oo, Platindr.
1o2 Timothy O'Sullivan, USA, Ruinen im Chelly-Canyon, 1873 Ap
1o3 Carleton E. Watkins, USA, Yosemite Valley, 1863 kol.Ap
1o4 Francis Frith, Die Wasserstraße nach Philae, 1859-6o, Ap
1o5 Camille Silvy, Fr., Flußszene, 1858 Ap
1o6 Friedrich Martens, Berglandschaft, ca 1855, Ap
1o7 Philipp H. Delamotte, Abend , ca 1854 Ap

Helmut Gernsheim, The Origins of Photography, Thames and Hudson, London 1982

1o8 Hippolyte Bayard, Blick auf die Rue Tholozé am Fuß der Windmühle "La Galette" 1843 Kalot.
1o9 Bayard, Gartenmauer, 1847 Kalot.
11o Bayard, Selbstporträt als Ertrunkener, 184o, Direktpos.
111 Talbot, Die Brücke in Orleans, 1843 Kalot.
112 Roger Fenton, Kuppeln der Auferstehungskathedrale im Kreml, 1852 Wachspapier
113 vermutl. Calvert Jones, Boote am Strand von Malta, Kalot. ca 1846, Collosseum in Rom, 1846, Kalot. 1846 Kalot.
114 John Shaw Smith, Relief am Tempel in Theben, 1851 Wachspapier
115 Alois Löcherer, Transport der Kolossalstatue der Bavaria, München 185o Wachspapier
116 Alois Löcherer, Transport der Kolossalstatue der Bavaria, München 185o Wachspapier
117 -- " --
118 John Whistler, Altes Bauernhaus, 1852 Wachspapier

Julia van Haaften, From Talbot to Stieglitz, London 1982

119 Maxime Du Camp, Baalbeck, Syrien, Kolonaden des Sonnentempels 1864 ca 185o
12o Du Camp, Palmen
121 Du Camp, Gesamtansicht von Kairo, ca 185o
122 Francis Frith, Kolossal-Skulpturen von Philae, 186o
123 Frith, Pyramiden von Sakkarah von Nord-Osten, 1858
124 Claude Joseph - Désiré Charnay, Gr. Palast in Mitla, Inneres des Hofes
125 Charnay, Gr Plast in Mitla, Gr. Saal, ca 1858
126 Louis-Auguste und Auguste- Rosalie Bisson, Ersteigung des Mont - Blanc, ca 1862
127 Charles Leander Weed, Zuckerhut, Kleines Yo-Semite-Tal, ca 1864/65

128 Weed Das Tal vom Mariposa Trail aus gesehen, ca 1864/65
129 CArleton E. Watkins, Teil des Grizzly-Riesen, Mariposa Grove, 1866
13o Watkkins, Spiegelblick, El Capitan, Yosemite, ca 1866
131 Samuel Bourne, Gwalidor, 186oer (Skulpturen)
132 Bourne, Die Schneeberge von Sandakfoo, Darjeeling, 186oer
133 John Thomson, Ruinen , City von Ayuthia, Alte Hauptstadt von Siam, ca 1866

134 Robert Demachy, Wald von Toucques, 1906

~~134 Alvin Langdon Coburn, Fountain Court, London, 1904-6 (Plowden, Landscape) Photogravüre~~

Jean - Luc Daval, Die Photographie, AArau, Stuttgart, 1983
DB 1983 B 3034

(135 W. Wiegand, Frühzeit der Photographie 1826-189o, Fr.M 198o)
Nicéphore Niépce, Blick auf den Hof seines Landhauses, 1826/27

136 Daguerre, Die Seine und die Tuilerien, 1839 Dag.
137 Bayard, Selbstporträt mit Statuen, Papierneg.
138 Talbot, Lektüre, 1841 Kalot.
139 Eugéne Durieu, Akt, 1853/54
14o Charles Nègre, Familie, ca 1855, im Freien vor einem aufgespannten Tuch aufgenommen, Kollneg.,Salzpap,
141 Le Gray, Ein Sonneneffekt - Ozean, ca 1856 Kollneg.
142 Durieu, Modell von vorn, ca 1853/54 Akt Salzpapierkopie
143 Maxime Du Camp, Karnak (Theben), Eingang zum großen Säulensaal, 1852 Papierneg.
144 Das Atelier Alinari, Florenz. Der Warte- und Poseraum 188o- 85 Gel.-Trockenplatte
145 Peter Osterhuis, Die Ankunft Nadars im Ballon am 14. Sept. 1865 in Amsterdam Koll.neg. Ap
146 Gardner (1821-82) Schlacht von Gettysburg, Juli 1863
147 Roger Fenton (1819-1869) Lager des 5. Regiments der Dragoner, Krimkrieg 1855
148 Nadar, Selbstporträt, ca 1854/55 Kollneg.Salzpap.
149 Nadar, Porträts von Honoré Daumier, 1855/56 Koll.neg.

Wilfried Wiegand, Frühzeit der Photographie, Frankf.M 198o

15o Southworth/Hawes, Unbekanntes junges Madchen, 1848 Dag.
151 Albert Sands Southworth, Selbstporträt als Büste, 1848 Dag.
152 (Charles Nègre, Kaminkehrer, 1852 Wachspapier
153 Stelzner, Das Ehepaar Daniel und Wilhelmine Runge, ca 1845 Dag.
154 Joseph Wilhelm Perxo, Die Lübecker Marienkirche, ca 1846 Dag.
155 Stelzner, Zwei Damen, 1848/49 Dag.
156, Stelzner, Mutter Albers, die Gemüsefrau der Familie, ca 1845 Dag.

157 Stelzner, Der Hamburger Künstlerverein, 1843 Dag.

158 Richard Beard, Jabez Hogg photographier Mr. Johnson, 1842/43 Dag.

159 An(Frk) Weiblicher Rückenakt, ca 1845

160 An (USA) Der Schmetterlingssammler, ca 1850 Dag.

161 Southworth/Hawes, Klassenraum einer Mädchenschule in Boston, ca 1855 Dag.

162 -- " --,Überschwemmung, ca 1855, Dag.

163 - " -, Niagara - Hängebrücke, 1855/56 Dag.

164 -"- , Bostoner Schönheit, ca 1850 Dag.

165 Anton Martin (Österr.), Winterlandschaft um 1841 Dag.

166 Gauklertruppe in Berlin, An. (Dt), 1846 Dag.

167 Charles Marville, Der Dom in Mainz von Südwest ca 1852 Dag.

168 Edouard Denis Baldus, Blick auf das Pariser Rathaus, ca 1860

Heinz Gebhardt, Königlich-Bayrische Photographie

169 Isenring, Barbara Tobler- Zellweger, vor 1846 kol. Talbot.

170 Johann Baptist Isenring, Porträt, Koll.neg., ca 1850 Kollneg. Carl Baumgartner 1847

171 Isenring, Katalog seiner Ausstellung 1840

172 Steinheil/Kobell, Bazaargebäude am Odeonsplatz 1839 Papierneg.

173 - " - , Glyptothek 1839 -"-

174 - " - , Frauenkirche von der Akademie der Wiss. aus gesehen, 1839 Papierneg.

175 Löcherer, Der 1844 gegossene Kopf der Bavaria im Hof der Erzgießerei

176 -"- , Ludwig von Schwanthaler, Ferdinand von Miller und Arbeiter der Erzgießerei nach dem Guß

177" Der Kopf der Bavaria vor ihrem Triumphzug zur Theresienhöhe 1850

178 - " - , Der Kopf der Bavaria auf ihrem Triumphzug zur Theresienhöhe, 1850

179 An.Dt., Dachauer Bauer, von einem Wanderphot. um 1850 phot. Dag.

180 An. Halbakt, Hälfte einer Stereoskopie, 50er JahreDt.,Dag.

181, Bayard, Wasserreservpor a, ?pmt,artre. 1845-50, Koll.neg. Ap.

Wiegand, Frühzeit der Phot.

182, Gebrüder Bisson, Der Ottheinrichbau des Heidelberger Schlosses, ca 1855

183 Gebrüder Bisson, Der Kölner Dom, 1855
184 - 2 -, Séracs du géant, Chemin du jardin,
Ein Gletscher am Montblanc, ca 1861

Gebhardt, Königlich-Bayr. Ph.
185 Löcherer, 1815-62, Selbstporträt Kol. Talbot.
186 - ", Familie Löcherer um 1857 im eigenen Studio,

Katalog Das Aktfoto, München 1985
187 An. Aufnahme, Kgl. Akademie der Künste, Berlin, Prof. J. Scheurenberg vor seiner Klasse ca 1900
188 Guglielmo Marconi, Akt, ca 1873
183 Paul Berthier, Akt, ca 1865
190 Hälfte einer anon. Stereodaguerreotypie, ca 1855, nach Perseus und Andromeda, koloriert
191 Rückenakt, Sterodag. ca 1855, Hälfte einer an. Stereodag.ca 1855
192 An (Fr.) Akt, Stereodag. ca 1850
193 Hermann Krone, Akt, ca 1850 Dag.
194 F.-Jacques Moulin, Doppelakt, ca 1855 Dag.
195 Felice Beato, Das Fort Bakou nach seiner Eroberung durch die alliierten Truppen Englands und Frankreichs, 1858

André Barret, Die ersten Photoreporter 1848 - 1914, Frankf.M 1978
196 , Eine Bootsbrücke in Khushalgar während der Besetzung Afghanistans durch drei engl. und ind. Armeekorps, 1878
197 An(Fr.) Aufmarsch der franz. Truppen auf den großen Boulevards anläßlich ihrer Rückkehr aus dem Italien-Krieg,1852 Dag.
198 T.O'Sullivan, General Grant (zweiter von links auf der Bank vor den Bäumen) und sein Stab, Massaponax Church, 1864
199 Wood und Gibson, Sonntagmorgen-Parade der Armee, Potomac, Mai 1862
200 Alexander Gardner, Leichte Artillerie bei der Belagerung von Petersburg, Virginia, Juni 1864
201 Mathew B.Brady, Die Trümmer eines Proviantwagens der Konföderierten, der am 3. Mai 1863 während der Schlacht von Chancellorsville zerstört wurde
202 R.Fenton, Viehtransport im Hafen von Balaklawa, 1855
203 James Robertson, Hafeneinfahrt von Balaklawa, 1855
204 R.Fenton, Die drei Oberbefehlshaber der Alliierten am Morgen der Eroberung von Memelon Vert am 7. Juni 1855
General Bosquet vor s.Zelt mit Hauptmann de Dampierre, 1855

Julia van Haaften, From Talbot to Stieglitz, London 1982

2o5 Baldus, Blick auf die Seine, ca 186o

2o6 Baldus, Palais Royal, Paris, ca 186o

2o7 Baldus, St. Eustache, Paris, ca 186o

2o8 Alexander Gardner, Ruinen des Arsenals von Richmond, Virginia, April 1863

2o9 Gardner, Studium der Kriegskunst, Fairfax Court House, 1863

21o George N. Barnard, Brücke bei Whiteside, 1864

211 George N. Barnard, Befestigungswerke der Konföderierten in Atlanta, 1864

Julia van Haaften, From Talbot to Stieglitz, London 1982

212 Etienne Carjat, Charles Baudelaire, ca 1853

213 Carjat, Henri Monnier, ca 186o

André Jammes, Hippolyte Bayard

214 Bayard, Aufnahme aus dem 5. Stock eines Hauses an der Rue Cambon, 1846 Ap

215 " , Dächer von Paris mit Blick auf die Vendome-Säule, 1845 Ap

216 " , Porträt einer unbekannten Dame, 1846/47

217 " , Eine Ecke in B-s Atelier, 1846-48 Ap

218 " , B als sein eigenes Modell, 1845-48 Ap

219 " , Bildkomposition mit Statuetten, 1839 Direktpos.

22o " , Dessin Photogéné, 1839 "

221 " , " 1839 - 41 Fotogramm

222 " , Blütenzweige 1839 Dir.pos.

223 " , Das Haus des Grafen de l'Escalopier, 1845-48 Ap

Werner Hofmann, Panorama einer Vergangenheit. Die ersten dreißig Jahre, Buchmuseum DB Leipzig

224 Talbot, Schluß Abbotsford, Sun Pictures in Scotland, 1844

225 Talbot, Walter Scott- Monument, Edingburgh, Oct. 1844, -"-

226 Talbot, Patroclus I, Pencil of Nature, 184o

227 Talbot, Patroclus II, - " - 184o

Hans Christian Adam, Fabian, Frühe Reisen mit der Kamera, Hamburg 1981 Buchmuseum DB Leipzig

228 William Henry Jackson, Felsformationen im Monument Park in Colorado, 1873

229 Carleton E. Watkins, Half Dome im Yosemite Valley, Cathedral Rock im Y. V., ca 1866

23o Eadweard Muybridge, Sentinel - Rock im Yosemite V., 1874

231 Muybridge, Spiegelung des Berges "El Capitan" im Merced-Fluß, 1874

232 Muybridge, Die Yosemite - Fälle, 1872

233 Jackson, Die Mammoth - Hot - Springs" im Yellowstone Nationalpark, ca 187o

234 John Thomson, Maler in seinem Atelier in Hongkong, ca 1868

235 Thomson, Frauenporträt ca 187o

236 Thomson, Chinesischer Kuli, ca 187o

237 Thomson, Stilleben mit exotischen Früchten, ca 1868

238 Thomson, Bettler in der Hafenstadt Futschou, ca 187o

239 Thomson, Kulis schürfen Kohle im Tagebau, ca 187o

Werner Hofmann, Panorama einer Vergangenheit. Die ersten dreißig Jahre, Buchmuseum DB Leipzig

240 Gustav Oehme, Berlin, Gruppenporträt, 1847 Dag.

241 Wigand, Berlin, Porträt (Herr mit Hund) ca 1850 Dag.

242 Kilburn, London, Stereoporträt eines Jungen, ca 1853 kol. Dag.

243 Lapanne, Paris, Zwei Kinder, ca 1850, kol. Dag.

244 An., Eichen im Wald von Fontainebleau, ca 1851 Kalot.

245 An. wahrsch. Gustave Le Gray, Gefallene Eichen, ca 1855 Salzpapier nach Wachspapier

246 Roger Fenton, Nubische Diener und Pferde, Krim 1855 Koll.

247 Fenton, Generalmajor Estcourt, Krim 1855, Koll.

Gernsheim, The origins of photography, London

248 An., Fra., Porträt eines Jungen, ca 1845 Dag.
249 An., Halbakt liegend auf einem Diwan, ca 1852,Stereodag.kol.
25o Leon Foucault, Trauben, 1844 Dag.
251 An., Fr., Garde im Hofgarten der Tulerien, 1842-8 Dag.
252 Hippolyte Fizeau, St. Louis-des-Invalides, da 184o Dag.
Girault de Prangey, Die Moschee von Kaaun in Kairo 1842 Dag.

AndréJammes, Hippolyte Bayard,

253 Bayard, Der Gendarmenturm in Caen, 1851 Koll.neg. Ap
254 " , Brunnen am Platz Notre Dame, 1847 "
255 " , Karren, 1842-45 "
256 " , Bildnis eines jungen Mädchens, 1845-48 "
257 " , B. in seinem Garten, 1845-5o "
258 " , Selbstbildnis in seinem Atelier, 1855-63 Ap

Gernsheim, The origins of photography, London
259 Daguerre, Boulevard du Temple, 1839 Dag.
26o " , Porträt eines an. Mannes, vielleicht Charles Arrowsmith, Assistent von D., ca 1842-3 Dag.
261 " , Notre Dame und das hist. Zentrum v. Paris 1838-9 Dag.
262 " , Stilleben, 1837, 1837 - 39 Dag.

Fritz Kempe, Daguerreotypie in Deutschland, 1979
263 Carl Ferdinand Stelzner, Familiengruppe, 1847 Dag.
264 Hermann Biow , Frau Susanne Hahn, ca 1784-186o, mit sieben von ihren 11 Kindern, 1843 Dag.
265 Biow, Wm. Campbell, 1843/44, Dag.
266 Biow, Dr. jur. Heinrich Nikolaus v. Beseler als Oberleutnant im Hamburger Bürgermilitär, 1843 Dag.
267 Biow, Abgeordneter C.Fuchs, Mitglied der National-versammlung Frankfurt, 1848/49 Dag.
268 Biow, Christian Rauch (1777-1857) 1847 in BerlinDag.
269 Biow, Jacob und Wilhelm Grimm, 1847.Berlin Dag.
27o Gustav Oehme, Bln, Gruppe Unbekannter, ca 1847 Dag.
271, Gustav Oehme, Bln, Drei unbekannte Mädchen,ca1845Dag.
272 J.W. Pero, Burgtor in Lübeck, vor 1847 Dag.
273 Stelzner, Johann Andreas von Bremen und seine Frau Wilhelmine und Tochter Minna, ca 1848 Dag.

274 Stelzner, Maria Taglioni (1804-84) Tänzerin Dag.

275 E. u. B. Wehnert, Gruppenporträt, 1845 Dag.

276 Josef Weniger (?), Familie Fixsen in St. Petersburg 1845 Dag.

277 Ed. und Bertha Wehnert, Lpg. Die Vorleserin, Mutter und Tochter, g.H. Dag.

278 (Clarence H. White, Morgen, 1906, Gummidruck über Platindruck

279 Stelzner, Caroline Stelzner, die Miniaturmalerin, erste Frau von St., (1808-79) 1843 Dag.

Beaumont Newhall, The daguerreotype in America

280 Alexander Hesler, Abraham Lindoln, Springfield 1860 Ap

Colin Ford, Portraits, London 1983

281 Southworth/Hawes, Bostoner Schönheit, 1850er kol. Dag.

282 Carroll, Alice Liddell als Bettler-Mädchen, 1862 Ap

283 Robert Howlett, Isambard Kingdom Brunel vor der Ankerkette der Great Eastern, 1857 Ap

284 Rejlander, Gustav Doré, 1868 Koll.neg.

285 Ghemar Frères, Verlobung des Prinzen of Wales mit der Prinzessin Alexandra von Dänemark, 1862, Salzpap.

286 Cameron, Paul und Virigina, 1865 Ap

287 Hill/Adamson, Lotse von Newhaven, 1845, Salzpap.

288 Baron Louis - Adolphe Humbert de Molard, Der Assistent des Fotografen als Gefangener, 1847 Dag.

289

290 Rejlander, Mr. und Miss Constable, 1866 Ap

291 John Jabez Edwin Mayall, Der Sprecher, ca 1865 Ap

292 Hill/Mc Glashan, Die Cousinen, 1862 Ap

293 Napoleon Sarony, Oscar Wilde, 1882 Ap

294 Mathew B. Brady, Robert E. Lee, Richmond, Virginia Ap 1865

295 M.B. Brady, Verwundete in Fredericksburg, ca 1862 Ap

Robert Doty, Photography in America, London 1974

296 M.B. Brady, Gefangenenlager von Konföderierten, Belle Plain, Virginia, ca 1962

297 G.N. Barnard, Ruinen des Eisenbahndepots Charleston 1865

298 G.N. Barnard, Befestigungswerke vor Atlanta, 1864

299 John Plumbe, Altes Patentamt, Washington D.C. ca 1846 Dag.

Newhall, The daguerreotype in America

300 George Read, Third Street in Chestnut, Philadelphia,
Juli 1842 Dag.
301 An., Chestnut Street, Philadelphia, ca 1844 Dag.
302 An., Zachary Taylor, 12. Präs. d. USA, ca 185o Dag.
303 An., John Tyler, 1o. Präs. der USA, ca 1845 Dag.
304 Sothworth/Hawes, Schlafendes Baby, ca 185o Dag.
305 An. Maungwudaus, Häuptling, Pennsylvania, ca 185o Dag.
306 An., Mädchenporträt ca 185o Dag.
307 An., Lokomotive "Hoosac" der Fritchburg-Eisenbahn
1854-62 Dag.
308 Southworth/Hawes, Schiff im Trockendock, Boston
ca1852 Dag.
309 An., Mrs Joseph Elisha Whitman und ihr Sohn Joseph
ca1854 Dag.
310 An., Hotelruinen in Buffalo N.Y., März 185o Dag.
311 An., Mutter und Kind, ca 185o Dag.
312 Southworth/Hawes, Unbekannter Mann, ca 185o Dag.
313 " , Lola Montez, ca 1852 Dag.
314 John Adams Whipple, Henry Wadsworth Longfellow,
ca 185o Dag.
315 An., Asher B. Durand, amerik. Maler, ca 1855 Dag.,
316 Henry N. oder Edward H. Manchester, Edgar Allan Poe, 1848
Dag.
317 William Shew , Fahrbarer Daguerreotyp-Wagen von
W. Sh., 1851 Dag.
318 An. Goldgräber, Kalifornien, ca 1852 Dag.
319 An., Yreka, Kalifornien, ca 185o Dag.
320 Southworth/Hawes, Lemuel Shaw, Hauptrichter von Massachusetts, 1851 Dag.
321 An., Caesar, der letzte Negersklave im Staat New Y.,Dag.
322 Southworth/Hawes, William Lloyd Garrison, Abolitionist, ca 185o Dag.
323 John Adams Whipple und James Wallace Black, John
Brown, Abolitionist, 1856/57 Dag.

Werner Hofmann, Panorama einer Vergangenheit. Die ersten dreißig Jahre, Buchmuseum DB Leipzig

324 James Robertson, Sebastopol, Krim 1855 Koll
325 Roger Fenton, E. Ross: Der Gewinner des Preises der Königin. (The Queens-Prize Schießwettbewerb, Wimbleton, 1860) Ap
326 Fenton, Schießscheibe des Schießwettbewerbs Wimbleton (des Siegers) 1860 Ap
327 Auguste Salzmann, Jerusalem, 1854 Kalot.
328 Salzmann, Jerusalem, 1854 Kalot.
329 Robert MacPherson, Relief am Titusbogen, Rom ca 1857 Ap
330 Charles Marville, Vierge Doreé, 1852 Kalot.
331 Ballerstaedt, Danzig, Turm "Kiek in de Kök", ca 1865 Ap
332 Hermann Krone, Basteibrücke, ca 1857 Ap
333 Krone, Basteihaus, ca 1857 Ap
334 Milton M. Miller, King of Siam, ca 1862 Ap
335 John Thomson, China, Fischer-Familie in Caton, 1869 Ap
336 Thomson, China, Hütte über dem Wasser, Canton, 1869 Ap
337 Thomson, China, Canton, Sonnenstrahlen im Tempel der 500 Götter, 1869 Ap
338 Krone, Dresden, Brühlsche Terasse, Belvedere, ca 1857Ap
339 Angerer, Wien, Theatergruppe, ca 1857 Ap
340 Thomson, Canton, Priester in Wha Lim Chee, ca1862Ap

Katalog Das Aktfoto, München 1985

341 An. Akademie, Akt ca 1865
342 Mustertafel für Akademien - Ausschnitt ca 1890
343 Eugène Durieu, Modell der Odalisque von E. Delacrois 1854
344 Clarence H. White, Akt, 1909
345 A. Calavas-Editeur, Männl. Akademien, ca 1900
346 A. Calavas-Editeur, Weibl. Akademien, ca 1900
347 An. Akademie (männl. Akt, ca 1880
348 Charles Simart, Männl. Akt, 1856 ca
349 G. Lambert, Singapur, Malaiin, ca 1890
350 Frank Eugene, Adam und Eva, 1898
351 Leopold Reutlinger, An. Halbakt, 1890
352 Anonyme Stereokarten (Akt) o.D.
353 An. Postkartenserie, Paris, Akt ca 1900
354 An. Aktaufnahme, verm. Dt. ca 1880
355 Zwei an. Stereodaguerreotypien Akt, ca 1855

356 Man Ray, Die Bitte (Gebet) La Priére, 193o
357 Imogen Cunningham, Akt, ca 193o
358 Edward Weston, Akt, 1935
359 Warwick Brookes GB, Eugen Sandow, ca 19oo (Akt)
36o Umbo (Otto Umbehr), Akt, 193o
361 Frantisek Drtikol, vor 193o, Akt
362 Franz Fiedler Ver Sacrum (Frühling) ca 1925 (Akt)
363 Man Ray, Demain (Akt) 193o
364xxLxWk
Newhall, Daguerreotype in America
364 L. Whright, Eisenbahnunglück der Providence-Worcester-
Linie nahe Pawtucket, 12.8.1853 Dag.
365 George N. Barnard, Brennende Fabrik in Oswego (New York)
5. Juli 1853 Dag.
366 John William Draper, Porträt seiner Schwester, Dorothy
Catherine Draper, Juni 184o Dag.
367 Katalog Aktfotografie, München 1985

367 Imogen Cunningham, Zwei Blumen, 1929, Silberbromid
368 Edward Weston, Akt, 1936 Gel - Silberbromid
369 Erwin Blumenfeld, Akt mit Schleier, Paris 1936 Silberbromid

Hans Christian Adam, Fabian, Frühe Reisen mit der Kamera,
Hamburg 1981 DB-Buchmuseum (kolor)

370 John Thomson, Porträt einer jungen Chinesin, ca 1868
371 " , Porträt einer vornehmen Chinesin, ca 1868
372 Samuel Bourne, Perlen-Moschee in Agra, 1865
373 " , Tor zum Basar von Lucknow, 1865
374 Studio Bourne &Shepherd (?) Der Maharadscha von Rewah
375 Samuel Bourne, Quelle des Ganges, 1866
376 Bourne, Bergpfand im Hamlaya, 1866
377 Marc Ferrez, Atelieraufnahme des Indianerhäuptlings Cumbo de Ucayale ca 1875
378 John Thomson, Jui Liu, Vizekönig der Kwang-Provinzen, ca 1871
379 Thomson, Der entblößte Lilienfuß, ca 1868
380 Marc Ferrez, Indianer vom Stamm der Botokuden in der Provinz Bahia, ca 1875
381 An, Japan, Das Bildnis auf der Haut (Rücken eines Mannes) ca 1880
382 An, Tanzunterricht in einer Geishaschule, ca 1900
383 An, Japan, Die menschliche Pyramide, ca 1890
384 Whrsch. Baron Stillfried, Akrobatenkind mit einem Kopfputz aus Federn, ca 1880
385 Kusakabe Kimbei, Akrobatische Übungen beim Neujahrsfest, ca 1890
386 whrsch. Baron Stillfried, Frauen mit Fächer, ca 1880 (Akt)
387 Baron Stillfried, Schlafende Frau auf Bastmatte, ca 1875 (Akt)
388 Kimbei, Buddistischer Mönch, ca 1885
389 whrsch. Baron Stillfried, Doppelporträt (Frauen) ca 1880
390 An., Japan, Harakiri im Fotostudio, ca 1890
391 Francis Frith, Kolosse in der Nubischen Wüste, 1857
392 Frith, Tempel auf der Insel Philae, 1857
393 Frith, Gestürzte Statue Ramses II in Theben, 1857
394 Frith, Säulenhalle in Karnak, 1857
395 Frith, Löwenkopf an der Außenmauer des Tempels von Denderah, 1857
396 Frith, Kloster St. Katharina in der Wüste Sinai, ca 1857
397 An., Japan Begrüßungszeremonie, ca 1885
398 Dunmore &Critcherson, Eisberge im Baffinmeer, 1869
399 " , Eisberge im Baffinmeer, 1869
400 " , Eisinsel im Baffinmeer, 1869

John Thomson, Street-life in London, London 1876,
Reprint Dortmund Harenberg Kommunikation 1981, DB SA 27o37-217

4o1 John Thomson, Nomaden
4o2 T., Droschkenkutscher,
4o3 T., Blumenverkäuferinnen, Covent Garden
4o4 T., Rekrutenwerber in Westminster
4o5 T.,Opfer der jährlichen Themseüberschwemmung
4o6 T., Entseuchungsdienst
4o6 T., Quacksalber
4o8 T., Plakatankleber
4o9 T., "Coney" (Korbflechter) ehem. Clown
41o T., Der abstinente Schornsteinfeger
411 T., "Tickets" (Schilder) ein Schildermaler
412 T., Altkleiderladen im Seven-Dials-Viertel
413 T., Besitzer einer Plakatfläche für Kleinanzeigen
414 T.,"BlackJack", Karrenhändler
415 T., Der eiserne Billy, ein Omnibuskutscher
416 T., Binnenschiffer auf der Themse
417 T., Londoner Plakatträger
418 T., Schirmflicker und Ginger-Beer-Verkäufer
419 T., Billiger Fisch im Viertel v. St. Giles
42o T., Haken-Alf, Gelegenheitsarbeiter von Whitechapel, seit einem Unfall ohne den linken Arm
421 T., "Die Kriechenden" (The Crawlers), Alte Frauen im Elend
422 T., Alte Möbel
423 T., Ein Schuhputzer ohne Lizenz

Ellen Maas, Die goldenen Jahre der Photoalben, Fundgrube und Spiegel von gestern, Köln 1977, DB 1977A 13519

424 Titelblatt eines Fotoalbums, 8oer Jahre
425 Atelier J.J. Tanner, Frankf.M, Kinder beim Fotografen 5oer J. mit Aquarellfarben übermaltes Salzfoto, Eingezeichnete Landschaft
426 Lederalbum mit Malereischmuck, ca 19oo
427 Album aus gepreßtem Kunststoff, rote Samtunterlage 6oer J.
428 Schmuckmotiv der 8oer Jahre:Landschaft, Fächer,Blumen Foto E. Bieber, Hamburg, ca 188o (Drei junge Frauen)
429 At. W. u.D. Downey, London, Prinzessin Louise Margarete v. Preußen, geb. 186o, März 1879
43o Totengedenkbild ca 19oo, in den Gebinden Haare des Verstorbenen, Foto 7oer Jahre
431 Aufstellalbum, Weinroter Samt, Mitte der 9oer Jahre
432 Stehalbum, Braunes Leder, Dt. Fabr., Foto:J.Black, Melrose 8oerJ
433 Mosaikfoto.Akte,3o Einzelaufnahmen 8oer Jahre
434 An., Dame, Arrangement mit Makartbouquet, ca 188o

435 An., Auf einem westfälischen Bauernhof (Porträt einer Bauersfrau oder Magd) 60/70er Jahre
An., Näherinnen auf einem Bauernhof (Aufnahme eines Wanderfotografen im Freien) 90er Jahre

436 Berufsdarstellungen, Visitformate 60er Jahre

437 Rudolf Rost, Darmstadt, Bauernfamilie ca 1900

438 Hofphotograph J.C. Schaarwächter, Blin, Kaiser Wilhelm mit Familie

439 St. Johann, Saarbrücken, Totenporträt (Großmutter) 90er J.

440 Franz Hanfstaengl, Carl-August von Steinheil

441 " , Dr. Gustav Scheve

442 " , Eduard Schleich d.Ä.

443 " , Heinrich Bürkel

444 " , Joseph Anton von Maffei

445 " , Jgnaz von Döllinger

446 " , Wilhelm von Kaulbach

447 " , Richard Wagner

Quelle Hanfstaengl: Christian Diener, Graham Fulton-Smith (Hrg.) Franz Hanfstaengl, Album der Zeitgenossen, München 1975 DB 1977B5266

Katalog Aktfoto, München 1985

448 Marsha Burns, Akt 1983

449 Lucien Clergue, Nus de la Mer, ca 1958

450 André Kertész, Distortion Nr. 126, 1931

451 Florence Henri, Akt mit Muschel, 1930

452 Bill Brandt, East Sussex Coast, 1959

453 Raoul Hausmann, Rückenakt, ca 1930

Maria Caronia, Vittorio Vidali, Peter Weiermair, Tina Modotti, Photographin und Revolutionärin, München 1981, ZB des VBK

454 Tina Modotti, Auf den Straßen von Mexico City, 1928

455 " , Callablüten, 20er J.

456 " , Landarbeiter, 1927

457 " , Frau mit Fahne, Mexico, 20er J.

458 " , Frau aus Tehuantepec, 20er J.

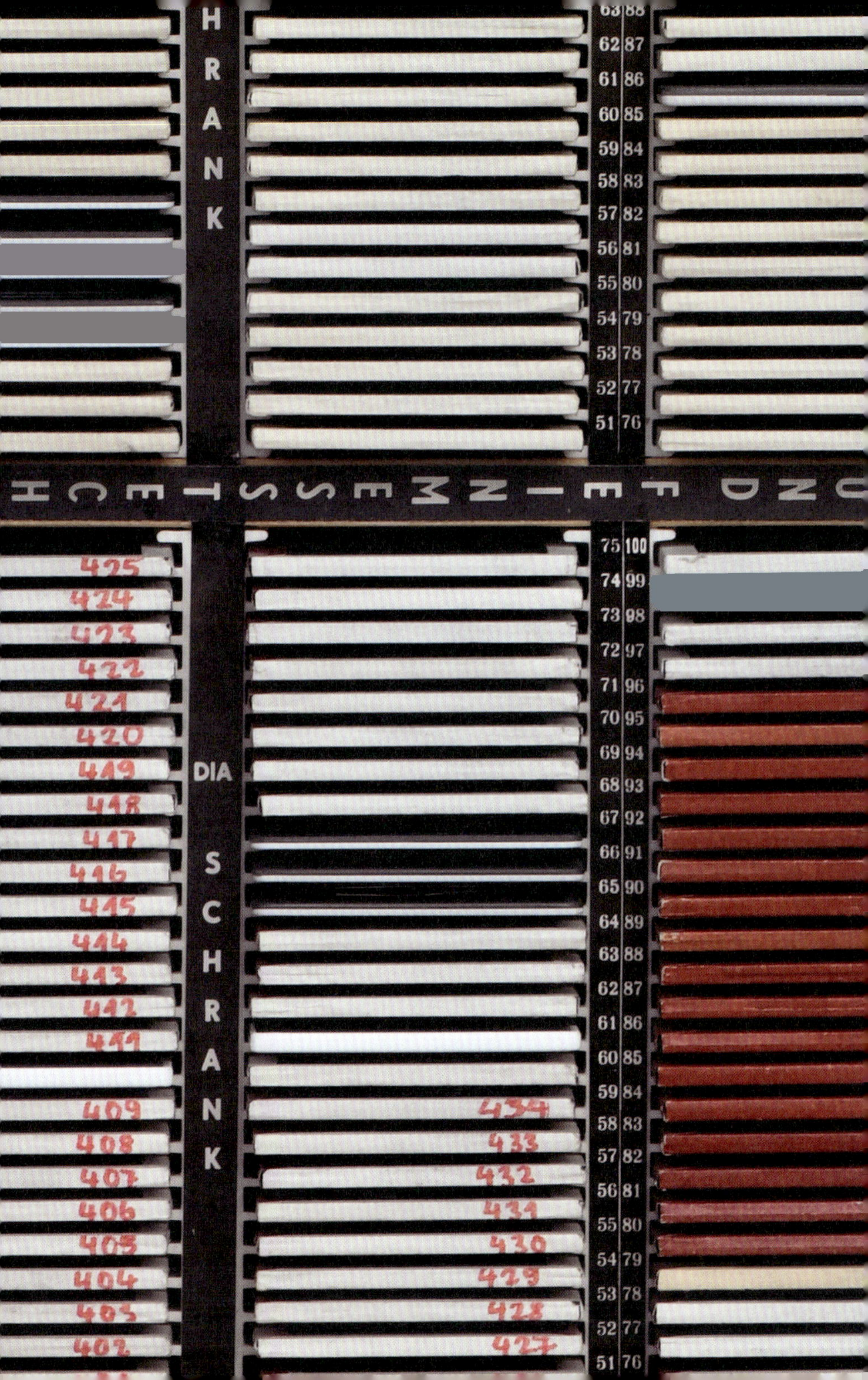
HRANK
DIA
SCHRANK

459 Tina Modotti, Schreibmaschine von J.A. Mella, ca 1928/29
460 Modotti, Terassen, Mexico
461 Modotti, Perspektive mit schwarzer Tür, Mexico City
462 Modotti, Torbogen mit Stiege, Mexico City
463 Modotti, Patronengürtel, Maiskolben und Gitarre
464

Charles R. Reynolds, Jr., American Indian Portraits from the Wanamaker Expedition of 1913, Brattleboro, Vermont, 1971
Stadtbib. Berlin

464 An., Boni - Titla, Indianer 1913
465 An., Bayard Looking Glass, Comanche, 1913
466 An., Haygivhu , Southern Cheyenne,
467 An., Three Fathers, Nez Percé,
468 An., Lizzie Hunter, Winnebago,
469 An., José Lupe Junior, Pueblo Isleta
470 An., Kowound Chippewa
471 An., Mother and Child, Havasupai
472 An., The boy Haskayelthnaga, Navajo
473 An., Susan Walser
474 An., Indian. Würdenträger, Pueblo
475 An., Juan Tres, Pueblo
476 An., Charles Shavanaux, Ute
477 An., Luoisa Impson, Choctaw
478 An., Juan de Jesus Pino
479 An., Hostino Bagota, Navajo
480 Am., David Neyos.
481xxxxxx

Katalog Aktfotografie, München 1985

481 Dieter Appelt, Aus der Serie "Erinnerungsspur - statische Vibrationen", 1977-79
482 Rudolf Schwarzkogler, II. Aktion "mit einem menschlichen Körper ", 1965
483 Pierre Boucher, Electra, 1936
484 Karel Teige, Fotocollage, 1947
485 Laure Albin-Guillot, Torso, 1939
486 George Platt-Lynes, Birth of Dionysus, ca 1937
487 Ruth Bernard, Doppelakt, 1963
488 Barbara de Genevieve, USA, Four Graces, 1979
489 Franklin C. Knott, Natives in French Guiana, ca 1910
490 An., Akt, Autochrome, ca 1910
491 Studio J. Mandel, Akt, Paris , ca 1920

492 An., Halbakt, ca 1925
493 Studio Manassé, Akt, ca 193o
494 Anton Sahm, Akt, ca 1925
495 André de Diénes, Shirley Levitt, ca 1945
496 Christian Vogt, Kim, 1981 (Akt)
497 Jeanloup Sieff, Paris, 1974 (Akt)
498 Wingate Paine, Aus der Serie "Mirror of Venus, ca 1965
499 Ilse Bing, Der Tänzer, 1932
5oo Arnold Genthe, Doris Humphrey, o.J.
5o1 Germaine Krull, Huldigung, 1924
5o2 Gerhard Riebicke, Diana, ca 1927
5o3 Kurt Teichert, Diskuswerfer, ca 194o
5o4 Benno Dahmen, Sergio Oliva, 1972
5o5 David Octavius Hill, Robert Adamson, D.O. Hill u. W. B. Johnstone, ca 1845, Calotype

John Szarkowski, Looking at photographs. 1oo Pictures from the Collection of The Museum of Modern Art, New York 1973, 4.Aufl.198o HGB

5o6 William England, GB, Niagara - Brücke, 1859
5o7 Nadar, Baron Isidore Taylor, ca 1865
5o8 Alexander Gardner, Heim eines Scharfschützen, Gettysburg, 1863
5o9 Julia Margaret Cameron, Madonna mit Kind, ca 1866
51o William McFarlane Notman, Schwarzfußindianer mit Pony, 1889
511 Peter Henry Emerson, Einbringen des Marschland - Heus, 1886
512 Henry Hamilton Bennett, USA, Sugar Bowl with Rowboat, Wisconsin Dells, ca 1889
513 Frances Benjamin Johnston, Landwirtschaft, Düngermischen, 1899/19oo Platindruck (Frau)
514 Arnold Genthe, Straße in Chinatown, San Francisco, ca 1896
515 Gertrude Käsebier, Die Kriegswitwe, o.D. Platindruck
516 Lewis Wickes Hine, Macon, Georgia, 19o9 (Kinderarbeit)
517 Jacques Henri Lartigue, Straße im Bois de Boulogne, Paris 1911
518 E. J. Bellocq, USA (Prostituierte) ca 1912
519 An., Lavannes, I. Weltkrieg, Luftbild, 1917

520 Edward Steichen, Säulen des Parthenon, 1921,Platindruck
521 László Moholy-Nagy, Ascona, 1926
522 Nickolas Muray, USA, Babe Ruth, ca 1927
523 Paul Strand, Giftpilz und Gräser, Georgtown, Maine 1928
524 Berenice Abbott, James Joyce, 1928
525 Imogen Cunningham, Blattmuster, vor 1929
526 Charles Sheeler, Kaktus und Photographenlampe, New York 1931
527 Erich Salomon, Französische Staatsmänner besuchen Berlin zum ersten Mal nach dem I. Weltkrieg 1931
528 Brassaï (Gyula Halász) Tanzsaal, 1932
529 Bill Brandt, GB, Junge Hausfrau in Bethnal Green, 1937
530 Arnold Newman, Porträt von Yasuo Kuniyoshi, New York 1941
531 Weegee (Arthur Fellig) Brooklinger Schüler sehen einen getöteten Spieler (Gambler) auf der Straße, 1941
532 Robert Capa, Kollaborateur, Chartres, 1944
and. Titel: Sie hat ein Kind von einem Deutschen
533 W. Eugene Smith, (USA) Dr. Ceriani, 1948
534 David Douglas Duncan, Capt. Ike Fenton, No Name Ridge, Korea, 1950
535 Irving Penn, USA, Frau in schwarzem Kleid, 1950
536 Frederick Sommer, USA, The Thief Greater than His Loot,1955
537 Richard Avedon, Isak Dinesen, 1958
538 William A. Garnett, USA, Death Valley, California 1957
539 Robert Doisneau, Im Café,Paris, 1958
540 Minor White, Capitol Reef (Rifi) Utah, 1962
541 Robert Frank, Political Ralley, Chikago, 1954
542 Naomi Savage, USA, Maske 1965 Fotogravure auf versilberter Kupferplatte, 1965
543 Diane Arbus, Pro War Parade, 1967

Kat.: Photographie als Kunst 1879-1979, Innsbruck 1979
Hrg. Peter Weiermair
544 Julia Margaret Cameron o.T.
545 Cameron, Der Friedenskuß
546 Cameron, Too Late! Too Late', 1868
547 Cameron, Im Garten

Marilies von Brevern, Künstlerische Photographie von Hill bis Moholy-Nagy, Bln, (W), 1971 Db SA 2o487 - 15 (16)

548 Carl Fredericksen, Kopenhagen, Nebliger Morgen, Platindruck
549 Rudolf Eikemeyer, New York, Die Trauernde, 19o2, Platindr.
55o Pierre Dubreuil, Lille, Ein Bildhauer, 19o2 Platindr.
551 James Craig Annan, (1864-1946) Die dunklen Berge, 1897/98
552 Frederick H. Evans, (1852-1943) Eine offene Tür (Kathedrale von Ely) Platinkopie
553 Minya Dièz- Dührkoop,(1873-1929) Prof Luksch und Frau 191o
554 Oskar und Theodor Hofmeister, Rechtsanwalt Wolters, 1899 Gummidr.
XXX Kevin MacDonnell, Der Mann, der die Bilder laufen ließ oder Eadweard Muybridge und die 25 ooo S - Wette
Luzern und Frankfurt 1973 DB 1973 B 1937
555 An, E. Muybridge, wahrsch. Universität v. Pennsylvania,1884/85
556 Muybridge, Bewegungsstudien, Animal Lokomotion
557 -- " --
558 .. " ..
559 -- " --
56o Thomas Eakins, 1885, Mehrfachaufnahme eines springenden Jungen
XXX Kat. Eadweard Muybridge, Stuttgart 1976, KDB
561 Muybridge, The Horse in Motion 1878
562 Muybridge, "Vernall Fall" o.D.
563

Kat. Photographie als Kunst 1879-1979, Innsbruck 1979 (Olbrich)
564 John B.B. Wellington (1858-1939) GB, Der Tod des Sommers ca 191o
565 Frances Benjamin Johnston (1864-1952) Motiv aus den Südstaaten, ca 19oo
566 Joseph Byron, (1846.1929(GB,ab 1888 USA) Handball am Lehrer-College, 19o4
567 Joseph Byron, Lebendes Bild, ca 19oo
568 Lewis W. Hine, 568 (1874-194o) Kinderarbeit in den USA 19o9/1o
569 Arnold Genthe (1869-1942) USA, Essenträger Chinatown, San Francisco, ca 19oo
57o Arnold Genthe, Das Erdbeben von San Francisco, 19o6
571 Fred Holland Day (1864-1933) Porträt einer Frau 19o7 USA
572 F.H. Day, (Bacchus) allgor. Darstellung o.D.
573 Wilhelm von Gloeden (1856-1931) Knabe, um 19oo
574 Gertrude Käsebier(USA) Mutter mit Kind, 19o1, Platindr.
575 James Craig Annan, Mädchen mit Blumen, o.D., Roter Gummidr.

Kunstphotographie um 19oo, Essen 1964 DB 1965 B 3o4o

576 Heinrich Wilhelm Müller (?) Segelboot, 19oo Blau-grüner Gummidr.
577 Robert Demachy, Tänzerin, O.D., grauer Gummidr.
578 Alexis Mazourine, Flußlandschaft mit Ruderboot, Platindr.
579 Nikolaus Perscheid, Bauer mit Sense, 19o1, blau-schw.Gummidr.
58o Henri Berssenbrugge , Aus Rotterdam, 19oo, Bromsilberdr.
581 Clarence H. White, Jungen, zur Schule gehend, 19o8, Heliogravüre
582 Th. u.O.Hofmeister, Bauernbildnis, Worpswede, Rot-Braun.Gummidr.
583 A. Böhmer, Vormorgen, 19o2, schw.-brauner Gummidr.
584 Frederick Hollyer (1837-1933)GB, Walter Crane o.D.
585 Julia Margaret Cameron (1815-79) GB J.F. W. Herschel 1867
586 Alexandre, Brüssel, Der Fischer
587 A. Böhmer, Ostseestrand, 1894
588 Otto Scharf (+1916) Pappeln am Fluß, 19o1
589 Gertrude Käsebier, (1852-1934) Die Skizze

Gesine Asmus, Hinterhof, Keller und Mansarde. Einblicke in Berliner Wohnungselend 19o1-192o, Reinbeck bei Hamburg
DB SA 128o3 - 7668

59o Berliner Wohnungsenquête, In einem Berliner Hinterhaus, 19o3
591 " , Wohnung unterm Dach, Friedrichstr. 236 19o4
592 " , Mansardenwohnung, Grenadierstr. 32 19o4
593 " , Heimarbeit, Quergebäude 3Tr., Liebigstr. 25 19o4
594 " , Liebigstraße 25 19o4
595 " , Wohnung im Keller, QG, Höchstestr. 18 19o5
596 " , Hof in der Höchstestr. 18 19o5
597 " , Kammer o.Fenster, Buckowerstr.14 19o5
598 " , Dachwohnung Prinz Handjerystr. 43 19o6
599 " , Küche von Lumpensammlern, Seestr. 27 19o9
" , DB ZC 15o2

6oo Die Woche, Berlin (Scherl)
Das neue amerikanische Kabinett Nr. 1, 19o1
6o1 DW Eine Künstlerfamilie: Maximilian von Heider mit seinen drei Söhnen Hans, Fritz und Rudolf
Die Werkstätte der Familie von Heider in Schongau am Lech 1/19o1
6o2 DW, Eröffnung der Verhandlungen im Preuß. Landtag am 9. Jan: Der neue Ministerpräsident Graf Bülow ergreift zum erstenmal das Wort 3/19o1
6o3 DW Augenblicksbilder vom Kriegsschauplatz in China 3 19o1
6o4 Vor der Deputiertenkammer in Paris: Henri Rochefort mit seinen Sekretären 8 19o1
6o5 DW Auguste Rodin (Meudon bei Paris 9 19o1
6o6 DW Burenkrieg: Generäle der Buren, 1901

607 DW Ein Blick i.d. Innenraum des neuen franz. U-Boots „Goubet" 1901

608 DW Neue Bilder aus China: Li Hung - Taschang empfängt in seinem Palast (Pekinger) unsern Photographen
Neue Bilder aus China: Silvesterfeier der 2.Kompanie des 5. Ostasiatischen Infanterieregiments in Tientsin 1o 19o1

609 DW Streik der Hafenarbeiter in Marseille: Hafenanlagen
" , :Die Streikenden verlassen die Ausladearbeit 11 19o1

61o Leipziger "Illustrirte Zeitung" Db ZD 386
Photographische Momentbilder vom Kaisermanöver bei Hamburg. Aufgenommen von Ottomar Anschütz, nachgebildet durch das Meisenbach'sche Hochdruckverfahren
LIZ 15.3.1884

611 ---- " ----

612 LIZ, 9.2.1884 Ein Arbeitermeeting in Batignolles, Paris Nach einer Skizze von St. Rejchan

613 LIZ 2.2.1884 Der Aufstand der pariser Lumpensammler Nach einer Skizze von St. Rejchan

614 LIZ Berliner Bilder: Ein Arbeitnachweisbureau. Originalzeichnung von C. Koch 12.4.1885

615 LIZ 31.5.1884 Der Brand des Stadttheaters zu Wien. Originalzeichnung von L.E. Petrowitsch

616 LIZ 21.6.1884 Mittsommer. Gemälde von Jan van Beers. Nach einer Photographie aus dem Verlage v.A. Block in Paris

617 Die Woche, Berlin, Vom Eisenbahnunglück bei Neuenbeken am 2o.Dez 1 19o2

618 DW, Die Kinder beim Korbflechten und bei häusl. Arbeiten 2 19o2

619 DW, Die Ankunft des Sühneprinzen Tschun in seiner Heimat: Der feierliche Einzug in Peking 3 19o2

62o DW Goldwäscher in Alaska 4 19o2

621 DW Aus Berliner Ateliers: Prof. Max Liebermann bei seinem neuesten Werk: Die Papageienallee im Amsterdamer Zoolog. Garten 4 19o2

622 DW Vom Brand des ~~Stadttheaters zu Wien~~ Stuttgarter Hoftheaters am 2o.Jan, Hans Hildenbrand, Stuttgart 5 19o2

623 DW Indien. Wie die Teeblätter sortiert werden 7 19o2

624 LIZ 2.1.1886 Ein photographirter Pferdesprung in zehn Augenblicksaufnahmen von Ottomar Anschütz in Lissa

625 LIZ 27.3.1886 Spielschrein. Geschenk des Vereins für deutsches Kunstgewerbe für das dt. Kronprinzenpaar zur Feier der Silbernen Hochzeit

626 LIZ 1.5.1886 Die Schießversuche gegen den dt. und franz. Panzerthurm bei Bukarest. Photografische Aufnahmen

627 LIZ 3.7.1886 König Ludwig II. auf dem Paradebett in der Alten Hofkappelle des Residenzschlosses zu München Originalzeichnung von J. Leonhard

Klaus-Jürgen Sembach (Hrg.) Amerikanische Landschaftsphotographie 186o - 1978, Katalog Neue Sammlung München, München 1979
DB 1979 B 129o

628 George N. Barnard, Chattanooga from the North, ca 1864
629 Timothy O'Sullivan, Eingang zum Black Canon, Colorado River, 1871
63o T.O'S., Südseite des Inscription Rock, 1873
631 E. Muybridge, Cottonwood Bend, Yosemite -Valley, 1872
632 William Henry Jackson, Berg des Heiligen Kreuzes,1879
633 W.H.J.,"Kathedralenspitzen" im Garden of the Gods, ca 1875
634 George Barker, USA, Niagara Falls, ca 1862

Olive Cook (Intr.) Edwin Smith - Photographs 1935 - 1971, London 1984, SLB 59 4° 1567

635 Edwin Smith, Neapel, April 1961
636 Straßenmarkt, Douglas Way, Deptford, London, 7.Dez 196o
637 Jahrmarkunterhalter, Micham, Surrey, August 1938
638 Laden in Florenz, Mai 1963
639 "Hof- Friseur", Dover Street, London, Juni 1935
64o Schachteingang, Ashington Colliery, Northumberland, August 1936
642 Die Themse bei Twickenham, März 1956
641 Kentish Town Station, London, Okt. 1936
643 Cod Wood, nahe Boyland, South Devon, Mai 1956
644 Ickworth House, Suffolk, Jan 1963
645 In Co. Donegal, Ireland Juni 1965
646 Bantry House, Co. Cork, Ireland, Mai 1965
647 Eine Turmtreppe, Château de Chambord, France Juli 196o
648 Farnblätter auf Mädchenrücken, Juli 1935 (Halbakt)
649 Linderhof, Baiern, Okt. 1966
65o Rousham, Osfordshire, Mai 1966
651 Isola Bella, Lago Maggiore, It. März 196o
652 Versailles, Fr. Juli 1962
653 Die Grotte, Clandon Park, Surrey, Sept. 1958

Julia van Haaften, From Talbot to Stieglitz, HGB
654 Alfred Stieglitz (1864-1946) Hände von Georgia O'Keefe ca 1918, Silver Print
655 --- " ---
656 Edward Steichen (1879-1973) Alfred Stieglitz, 19o5 Platindr.
657 Frank Meadow Sutcliffe, (1853-1941 GB) Laß uns mitfahren, 188oer, Carbondr.

658 Frank Meadow Sutcliffe, Badende, 188oer Carbondr.
659 Edward Sherriff Curtis (1868-1952 USA) Housetop-life-Hopi ca 19oo. Silverprint
66o Curtis, Canon del Muerte - Navajo, ca 19oo, Silverprint
661 John K. Hillers, (USA, geb. in Deutschland, 1843-1925). Zuni Watching, ca 1875 Albumenprint

Paul Brooks, Ansel Adams. Yosemite and the Range of Light, Boston 1979, DB BuMu VI 274 USA

662 Bergspitzen und Wiese, Gableung des Merced River, Yosemite Nat. Park 1943 ca
663 Toter Baum, Hundesee, Yosemite, 1933
664 Friedhofstatue und Öltürme, Long Beach, Californien, 1939
665 Brassai, Yosemite, Cal., 1973
666

Wallace Stegner (Ed.) Ansel Adams. Images 1923 - 1974, New York Graphic Society, Boston, Massachussetts 1974, DB BuMu

666 A. Stieglitz und O-Keefes Gemälde " An American Place" New York City, N.Y., ca 1939
667 Mannequins, Columbia Movie Lot, Los Angeles, Ca., ca 194o
668 Kirche und Straße, Bodega, Cal., ca 1953
669 Hausruinen, Canyon de Chelly, Arizona 1942
67o St.Francis Church, Ranchos de Taos, New Mexico, ca 1929
671 Mondaufgang, Hernandez, New Mex., 1944
672 Vereister See und Klippen, Sierra Nevada, Cal. , 1927
673 Mount Williams, Sierra Nevada, 1944
674 Bäume nahe Washburn Point, Yosemite Valley ca 1945
675 Monolith, Vorderseite des Half Dome, Yosemite, 1927
676 Gletscher, Milestone Ridge, Sequoia Nat. Park, ca 1927
677 Segoia, Rinde, ca 1954, Yos. Nat.Park, ca 1954
678 Hochland, Felsen und Mond, Sonnenaufgang, Kings Canyon Nat. Park, ca 1935
679 Mount Clarence Königssee, Kings Canyon Nat. P. ca 1925
68o Mond und Half Dome, Yosemite V. 196o
681

Florence Durtis Graybill und Victor Boesen, Ein Denkmal für die Indianer. Edward Sherriff Curtis und sein photographisches Werk, München 1979, DB BuMu 1981 B 5631

681 Curtis "Mosa", Mohave-Mädchen

682 Curtis, Gebet der Oglala Sioux
683 Curits, "In die Hand geschossen", Apsaroke
684 Curtis, "Zwei Gamaschen" Apsaroke-Indianer
685 Curtis, Bemalung eines Hutes, Nakoaktok- Indianerin
686 Curtis, An der Quelle v Acoma
687 Curtis, Bemaltes Tipi der Assiniboin

Werner Hofmann, Panorama einer Vergangenheit. Die ersten 3o Jahre 184o - 187o, Hamburg 1982, DB BuMu

688 Christian Friedrich Brandt (1823 - 1891) Dt-dän. Krieg, Düppeler Schanzen, April 1864
689 Joseph Albert (1825 - 1886) Deutscher Fürstenkongreß, Frankfurt a M., 1.9.1863
69o Paul Sinner (Tübingen) Laborwagen des Photographen in Straßburg, Sept. 187o nach der Eroberung durch die dt. Truppen
691 Sinner, Straßburg, Sept. 187o
692 E. Robert (o.D.) Zerstörte Häuser in St. Cloud, Paris, 1871
693 Franck (Francois-Marie-Louis-Alexandre Gobinet de Villecholle, (1816-19o6) Paris, Place Vendome, 1871

Winfried Ranke, Heinrich Zille. Photographien Berlin 189o-191o. München, 1975, DB 1976 A 1oo4

694 Zille, Zilles Eltern vor ihrem Haus in Rummelsburg ca 189o
695 Zille, Aktstudie im Atelier von August Gaul, ca 19oo/o3
696 Aktstudie, ca 19oo
697 Wilhelm Knötzsch, Destillation
698 Arbeiter auf dem Heimweg, Carlottenburg, ca 19o2
699 Auf einer Kreuzung der Friedrichstraße
7oo Pelze und Rauchwaren
7o1 Frauen beim Einkaufen, Charlottenburger Markt, ca 19oo
7o2 Berlin - Dircksenstraße
7o3 Produktenhandlung Minna Neumann, Bln- Parochialstraße ca 19oo
7o4 Beerdigungsinstitut Aßmann, Bln, Bergstraße 64, ca 191o
7o5 Charlottenburg, Friedrich-Karl-Platz, Frauen beim Einkaufen ca 19oo
7o6 Frauen mit Holzfuhre, ca 19oo
7o7 Frau mit laubgefüllter Kiepe, ca 19oo
7o8 Wäschetrockenplatz in Charlottenburg
7o9 Hunde-Theater, Charlottenburg
71o Herausforderung (Rummel)

711 Heinrich Zille, Einsames Paar (Rummel)
712 Putzgerüste im Hof des Charlottenburger Wohnhauses, o.D.
713 Pinkelnder Knabe (Walter Zille) ca 1901/02
714 Zille mit seinen Söhnen im Freibad Charlottenburg
715 Atelierfest bei dem Maler Walter Meyer, Lübeck, 17.12.1899
716 Aktstudie im Atelier August Gaul
717 Aktstudie im Atelier August Gaul
718 Aktstudie im Atl. August Heer
719 Aktstudie, ca 1900
720 Krögelgasse nach Norden
721 Hausdurchgang am Krögel, ca 1900
722 Umzug im Scheunenviertel

Günter Metken, Herbert List. Photographien 1930 - 1970, München 1976, DB 1976 B 2820

723 Herbert List,
Ostsee bei Lübeck ca 1930
724 Ostsee (Porträt) 1933
725 Rostock - Stralsund (?) 1934
726 London 1936
727 Portofino, 1936
728 Santorin, 1937
729 Griechenland, 1939
730 Paris 1937
731 Santorin 1937
732 Lykabettos, 1937
733 Athen, 1937
734 Neapel, 1961
735 Georges Huyningen- Huené, Glyphada 1937
736 Korfu 1938
737 Spakia, Kreta (?) 1937
738 Korfu 1938
739 München 1945
740 München 1946
741 Paris 1936

742 D'Ora, Die Revuetänzerin Josephine Baker, 1928
43 d'Ora, Montmartre - Friedhof, 195o
44 d'Ora, Madame Rupert, ca 1953
45 d'Ora, Schlachthofserie, Geschlachteter Hase, vor 1958
46 d'Ora, Schlachthofserie, Aufgehängte Schafsköpfe mit Lupe
47 Hill/Adamson, James Linton, Newhaven
48 Edouard Denis Baldus, Die Bibliothek des Louvre, 1855
49 Lewis Carroll, Alice Liddell, 1859 , Albumin
750 Stieglitz, Georgia O'Keefe, 1923
51 Stieglitz, Äquivalent, 1925
52 Emil Otto Hoppé (1878-1972), Porträt des Schriftstellers Arnold Bennett 1911
53 Hoppé, Öltanks in Berlin 1928
54 Cecil Beaton (19o4-198o) Nancy Beaton 1926
55 Erwin Blumenfeld 1897-1969, Nasser Schleier II 1937 (Akt)
56 Blumenfeld, Schönheit mit Rehaugen, 1956
57 Brassai, (Guyla Halasz) 1899-, Prostituierte am Billard-
tisch
58 Brassai, Zwei Apachen 1932
59 Irving Penn, Lisa Fonssagrives, 1950 (fashion)
760 Imogen Cunningham (1883-1976) Der Traum, 191o
61 Atelier d'ora-Benda, Der Dichter Hermann Bahr, 19o9
62 - " - , Hut, entworfen vom Maler Kreiser, Wien
63 - " - , Alma Mahler-Werfel, 19o9
64 - " - , Karl Kraus, 19o8
65 Nicola Perscheid, Frl. Sakur, ca 19o5
66 Perscheid, Max Klinger, 19o2
67 Florence Henri, Robert Delaunay, 1934
68 Florence Henri, Frauenbildnis, ca 193o
69 Henri, Porträt-Komposition, ca 193o
770 Henri, Zwirnrolle, 1928
71 Henri, Rom (Fotomontage, 1936
72 Henri, Pariser Fenster, 193o
73 Herbert List, Giorgio de Chirico, Rom 1951
74 List, Giorgio Morandi, Bologna 1953

Quellen: Fritz Kempe, Nicola Perscheid, Arthur Benda, Madame d'Ora, Hamburg 198o, DB SB 9145 - 1
Herbert Molderings (HRG), Florence Henri, Aspekte der Photographie der zwanziger Jahre, Münster/Baden-Baden 1976, DB
Brian Coe, David Allison ua. Foto Genies, Derendingen-Solo thurn 1983 DB 1984 B 695

Dias Fotogeschichte

Margery Mann (Introd.) Imogen ! Imogen Cunningham Photographs 191o-1973, Seattle, London 1974, Stabi 7 - 32 SB 163-7

775 Imogen Cunningham (1883-1976) The vision, 191o
76 Cunningham, On Mount Rainier I, 1915 (Akt)
77 Cunningham, - " - III,1915
78 Cunningham, Edward Weston and Margrethe Matker, Photographers I, 1923
79 Cunningham, Sherwood Anderson, 1927
780 Cunningham, Martha Graham 2, 1931, Doppelbelichtung
81 Cunningham, - " - 4,
82 Cunningham, Agave Design I , 192oer
83 Cunningham, - " - " ,
84 Cunningham, Ansel Adams, 1953
85 Cunningham, Brassai, 1971
86 Cunningham, Hands and Aloe plicatilis, späte 6oer
87 Cunningham, Ein anderer Arm, 1973
88 Cunningham, Selbstporträt, 1972
89 Cunningham, Meine Signatur, 1973
790 Atelier d'Ora-Benda, Die Operettendiva Fritzi Massary, 1923

Hannes Maria Flach. Photographien der zwanziger Jahre, Köln 1983 (Katalog), Stabi 37 MB 852

791 Hannes Maria Flach (19o1-1936, Selbstporträt als Rufer
92 Flach, Frauenporträt
93 Flach, Hohenzollernbrücke in Köln mit Groß St. Martin,1928
94 Flach, Eisen, Hohenzollernbrücke in Köln
95 Flach, Hohenzollernbrücke mit Blick auf den Kölner Dom
96 Flach, Berlin, Friedrichstraße
97 Flach, Blick vom Dachreiter des Kölner Doms rheinwärts
98 Flach, Blick auf das Kölner Domhotel
99 Flach, Kölner Dom, Gotik-Technik
800 Flach, Südturm mit Kreuzblume
01 Flach, Hängebrücke mit Sandstrahlbläsern
02 Flach, Berlin, U-Bahn
03 Flach, Kölner Bücherei
04 Flach, Spinnmaschine
05 Flach, Frau mit Flugzeug
06 Flach, Porträt mit Linse

807 Flach, Radio- oder Weltenwerke, Fotogramm
808 Flach, Komposition, Fotogramm

Andreas Haus, Moholy-Nagy.Photographs and Photograms, London 198o bzw. München dt. 1978, ZB des VBK

809 Lászlò Moholy Nagy (1895-1946) (liegende Puppe) 1926
10 (Kinder) 1926
11 Dessau 1926-28
12 Lyon ca 1929
13 Belle-Ile-en-Mer, 1925
14 Paris 1925
815 Berlin ca 1928
16 Berlin 1928 (Blick vom Funkturm)
17 Marseille 1929
18 ca 1927 (Negativ)
19 Porträt Ellen Frank ca 1929
820 Porträt
21 Porträt (einer alten Frau) Positiv
22 Porträt (einer alten Frau) Negativ
23 (Akt) Negativ, 1927-29
24 Katze, Negativ ca 1926
825 Paris 1925 (Rinnstein)
26 Porträt 193o
27 (Lichtmodulator) 1922-3o
28 Fotogramm, 1922 (?)
29 Fotogramm, 1922-23
830 Fotogramm 1923
31 Fotogramm 1922
32 Fotogramm 1925-27
833 Fotogramm ca 1928

Ute Eskildsen, Horak, Film und Foto der zwanziger Jahre, Stuttgart 1979, Stabib

834 Plakat der Ausstellung "Film und Foto" Stuttgart 1929

Erika Billeter (HRG) Amerika-Fotografie 192o-194o, Hannover 198o Stabib

835 James Abbe (1883-1973) Fred und Adele Astaire,New York 1921
36 Abbe, Rudolph Valentino, New York 1922
37 Clarence Sinclair Bull (1896-) Greta Garbo
38 Bull, Greta Garbo als Camille
39 George Hoyningen-Huene (19oo-1968) Ava Gardner
840 Huene, Marlene Dietrich
841 Horst P. Horst))(19o6-) Marlene Dietrich, 194o

842 Hoyningen-Huene, Greta Garbo
843 Barbara Morgan (1900-) Martha Graham, Letter to the World 1940 32
844 Morgan, American Dokument, (Puritan Love Duet) with Erick Hawkins, 1938
845 Hoyningen-Huene, Lily Damita, 1933
Dias Fotogeschichte

Katalog Photographie als Kunst 1879-1979, Innsbruck 1979

846 Wilhelm von Gloeden (1856-1931) (Knabe) ca 1900
47 Gloeden, Knabe mit Flöte
48 Fred Boissonnas (1858-1946)Schweiz, Dalcroze-Schule,Hellerau
49 Robert Demachy (1859-1938)Dt., Lesendes Kind
850 Demachy, Auf dem Sand
51 Frederick Evans (1853-1943) GB, Westminster No.17
52 Clarence Hudson White (1871-1925)USA,Mädchen im Wald,1909
53 White, The Venetian blinds
54 White, Regentropfen 1912
55 Gertrude Käsebier (1852-1934) Porträt
56 Eva Watson-Schütze &1867-1935) USA, Die Lilie
57 Heinrich Kühn (1866-1944) Glas, ca 1900
58 ~~Alfred~~ Kühn, Alfred Stieglitz, ca 1904
59 Kühn, Edward Steichen,ca 1907
860 Kühn, Stilleben ca 1900
61 Kühn, Dame in Landschaft, ca 1905
62 Hugo Henneberg (1863-1918), Portrait eines jg. Mädchens
63 Henneberg, Motiv bei Stillfried (Ldsch)
64 Hans Watzek (1848-1903) Vanitasstilleben, 1895
65 Watzek, Fingerspitze (Tirol) 1893 (Gebirge)
66 Ludwig David (1856-1930) Dt.Österr., H. Henneberg 1901
67 Frank Eugene (1865-1936) Frau Ludwig von Hohlwein, 1910
68 Eugene, Akt - eine Studie, 1910
69 Eugene, Eine Gruppe von Fotografen re-links: Steichen, Kühn Stieglitz, Eugene
870 Eugene, H. Kühn
71 James Craig Annan (1864-1946) Das weiße Pferd , 1890
72 Edward Steichen (1879-1973) Mrs.Conde Nast, Paris, 1907
73 Steichen, Portrait der Schwester Milwaukee, 1899
74 Alvin Langdon Coburn,(1882-1966) Schatten u.Reflexe,Venedig 1905
75 Coburn, London Houses of Parliament
76 Frederick Henry Evans (1852-1943)GB, Aubrey Beardsley
77 Henri Berssenbrugge (1873-1959) Holl, o.T.(Spital) 1904
78 Rudolf Dührkoop (1848-1918) Bildnis eines Mädchens 1912
79 Alfons Mucha (1860-1939) Paul Gauguin, ca 1900
880 Mucha, Aktstudie

John Kobal (Ed.), Hollywodd Glamour Portraits.145 Photos of Stars 1926-1949, New Aork 1976 HGB

881 A.L. "Whitey" Schaffer beim Lichteinstellen für ein Porträt von Dolly Haas, 1937 (Columbia)

882 Apeda, New York, Marion Davis, 1928

883 Eugene Robert Richee, Louise Brooks, 1928

884 Don English, Clara Bow, 1928

885 Nelson Biddly Keyes, Jetta Goudal, 1924

886 Cecil Beaton, Evelyn Brent, 1930

887 George Hurrell, Jean Harlow, 1932

888 Hurrell, Jean Harlow, o.D.

889 Hurrell, Joan Crawford, o.D.

890 Hurrell, Joan Crawford, o.D.

891 Don English, Marlene Dietrich, 1932

892 E.R.Richee, Carole Lombard, 1935

893 Ernest A. Bachrach, Ann Harding, 1933

894 Clarence Sinclair Bull, Gary Cooper, 1934

895 George Hurrell, Johnny Weissmuller als Tarzan, 1933

896 Hurrell, Robert Montgomery, 1932

897 Bachrach, Katherine Hepburn, 1935

~~898 C.S.Bull, Greta Garbo, 1931~~

~~899 Bull, Luise Rainer, 1935~~

~~Rub~~

Helmut Gernsheim, (Intr.) Lewis Carroll, London 1980, Stabi 8-36 MA 2252

898 Ella Balfour

899 Katie Brine, Enkelin von Dr. Dusey, Dean der Christ Church

900 Beatrice Henley, Tochter des Vikars von Putney

901 Xie Kitchin, Tocher von Rev. George William K.

902 Xie Kitchin, ca 1875

903 Alice Liddell, Tochter des Dean der Christ Church

904 Irene Mac Donald

905 Mary Millais, Tochter von John Everett M.

906 Polly und Terence Terry, jüngere Schwestern von Ellen Terry

907 Evelyn Wilson

908 Lizzie Wilson

Brassai, The artists of my life, London 1982, HGB

909 Brassai (Gyula Halász (1899 -) George Braque in seinem Atelier, Impasse du Douanier, 1935/36

910 Dali, einen Fischerkorb haltend, wie Atlas die Welt trägt, 1955
911 Dali malend in seinem Atelier in Port Lligat 1955
912 Raoul Dufy malend, 1949
913 Alberto Giacometti in der Tür seines Ateliers 1948
914 In G.s Atelier, 1948
915 G.: "L'Objet Invisible" 1934-35
916 Kokoschka, ca 1931/32
917 Henri Laurens Atelier, 1946
918 Laurens mit seiner Skulptur "Große Musikerin" 1946
919 Le Corbusier, 1952
920 Fernand Leger, Paris 1937
921 Jacques Lipchitz' Atelier, Boulogne-sur-Seine-Billancourt,1932
922 Aristide Maillol beim Arbeiten an "L'Ile de France", ca 1932
923 Maillol mit "Das Gebirge" 1936
924 Maillol an seinem 75. Geburtstag, 1936
925 Henri Matisse in seinem Atelier, 1939
926 Matisse beim Aktzeichnen, 1939
927 Picasso und seine Frau Olga, Château de Boisgeloup, 1932
928 Matisse beim Zeichnen, 1946
929 In Matisse's Villa "Le Rêve" in Vence, 1946
930 Juan Miró neben der Leinwand mit seinen Handabdrücken, 1955
931 Miró im Güell Park von Gaudy, 1955
932 Picasso in seiner Wohnung, Paris, 1932

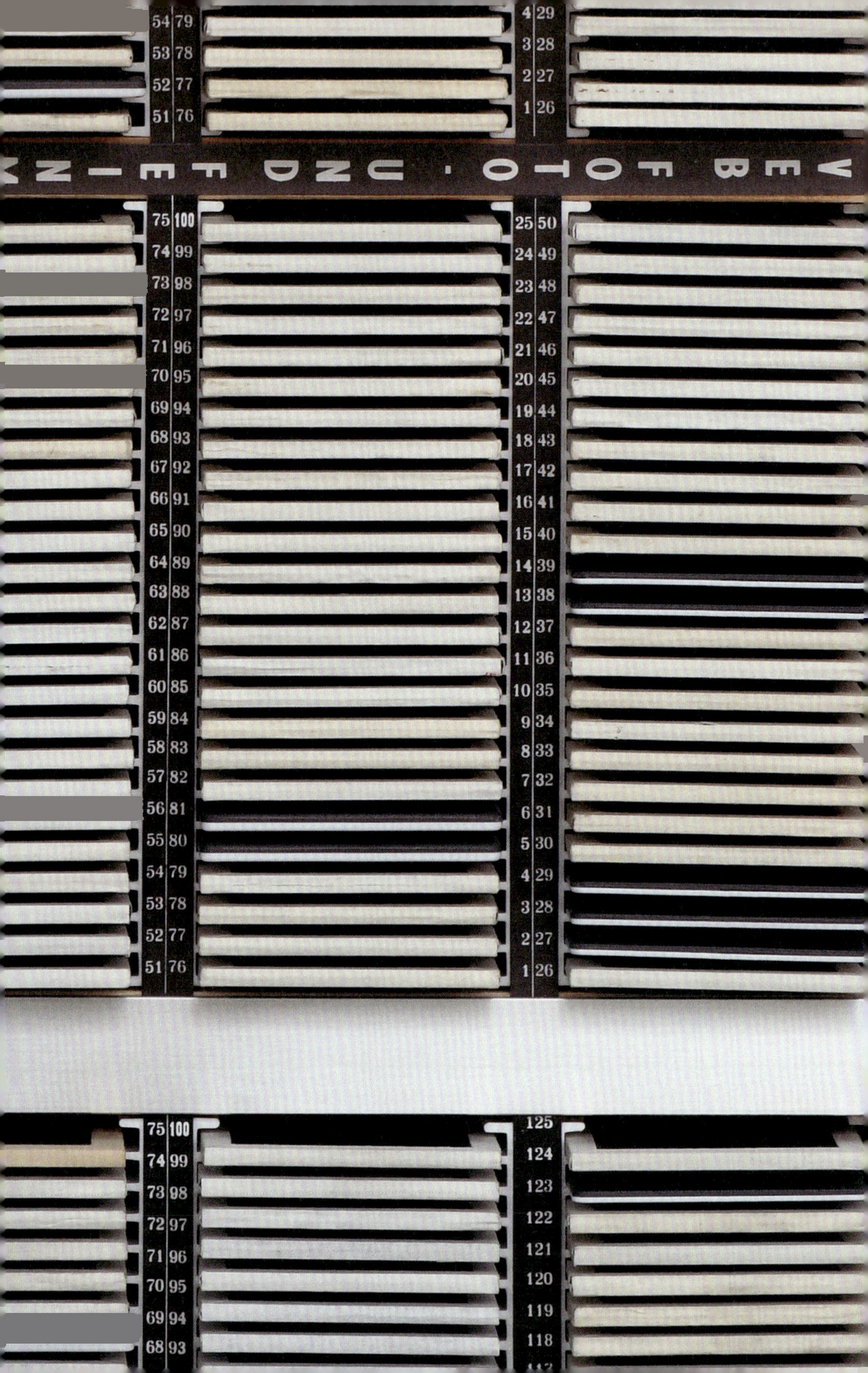

Dias Fotogeschichte

933 Brassai, Picassos Atelier nachts, Châtequ de Boisgeloup,1932
934 Brassai, Picasso mit Pierre Matisse, dem Sohn des Malers, in der Brasserie Lipp, 1939
935 Picassos Hand, 1943
936 Picasso im Atelier, Paris 1939
937 Dora Maar, 1944
938 Germaine Richier an ihrer Druckpresse, ca 1955
939 Germaine Richier beim Arbeiten an einer Skulptur, ca 1955
940 Jacques Villon in seinem Atelier in Puteaux, 1954
941 Daniel - Henry Kahnweiler neben Picassos "Der Engel" auf
942 seinem Besitz Le Prieuré de Saint-Hilaire, 1962
943 Ambroise Vollard, 1934

Kat. Photographie als Kunst

943 Edward Sherriff Curtis (1868-1952) Hopi-Mann, 1921
944 Francis Bugière(1880-1945) Apartement
945 George Hoyningen-Huene (1900-1968) Gustav Gründgens, 1932
946 Hoyningen-Huene, Josephine Baker, 1931
947 Hoyningen-Huene, Madame Munoz
948 Horst P. Horst (1906-) Modephotographie, 1938
949 Cecil Beaton (1904-1980) Edith Sitwell, 1962
950 George Platt-Lynes (1907-1955) o.T. (Männerakt)
951 ----- " ----
952 ----- " ----
953 György Kepes (1906-1984?) Juliet mit einem Pfaunfederauge, 1938
954 Raoul Hausmann, Der Traum/Deutschland, 1931
955 Hausmann, Akt
956 Hausmann, Akt
957 Hausmann, Fotogramm
958 Christian Schad (1894-1982?) Schadographie
959 Herbert Bayer (1900-1985) Photoplastik, 1936
960 Bayer, Photoplastik
961 Werner Mantz (1901-) Titelbaltt Programmheft WDR 1928
962 Karl Blossfeldt (1865-1932) Dipsacus lacinatus, Weberdistel
963 Blossfeldt, Acanthus mollis, 1900-28
964 Blossfeldt, Papaver orientale, 1900-28
965 Margarete Bourke-White, 1904-71, Skikorsky-Propellor, o.D.
966 Bourke-White, Minenarbeiter Südafrika, 1950
967 Florence Henri, 1895-) Porträt, o.D.
968 Erwin Blumenfeld, 1900- (verhälltes Gesicht) 1930

969 Blumenfeld, o.T. (Porträt) 1933
97o Imogen Cunningham (1883-1976) Magnolienblüte, 1925
971 Edward Weston (1886-1958) Akt, im Wasser treibend, 1939
972 E. Weston, Kirchentür, oD.
973 Weston, Muschel, 1927
974 Weston, Paprika, 193o
975 Theo van Doesburg 1883-1931,(Porträt-Interieur) 1925
976 Hugo Erfurth (1874-1948) Dame, ca 191o
977 Adolf de Meyer, (1868-1949) Gloria Swanson
978 de Meyer, Berthe, Modell stehend, ca 1918
979 de Meyer, Helen Lee Worthing, Revuestar, 192o
98o de Meyer, Ruth St. Denis, Tänzerin
981 de Meyer, Lady Ottoline Morrell, 1912
982 de Meyer, Alvin Langdon Coburn
983 de Meyer, Elisabeth-Arden, Reclame
984 de Meyer, Marchesa Casati, ca 1912
985 de Meyer, Nijinsky in "Schéhérazade" London 1911
986 de Meyer, Rita de Acosta - Lydig
987 De Meyer, Frühes Selbstporträt,
988 Robert Brandau , De Meyer, London 1976, HGB

Hollywood portraits

988 A.L. Schafer, Corinne Calvert, 1948
989 Ernest A. Bachrach, Gloria Swanson, 194o
99o Robert Coburn, Barbara Stanwyck, 1937
991 Coburn, Merle Oberon, 1938
992 Clarence Sinclair Bull, Louise Rainier, 1935
993 Bull, Greta Garbo, 1931
994

994 Werner Mantz, Operationssaal, 1928
995 Walter Peterhans (1897-1960) o.T. (Stilleben)
996 Frantisek Drtikol (1883-1961) Mädchenakt
997 Drtikol, Portrait mit Hut (Akt)
998 Drtikol, Portrait der Schauspielerin Anna Sedlocková
999 Drtikol, Arbeiter
1000 Jaromir Funke (1896-1945) Komposition, 1925-28

Aenne Biermann.60 Fotos. Mit einer Einleitung von Franz Roh, Berlin (Klinckhardt und Biermann) 1930 HGB

1012 Aenne Biermann (1898-1933) Nadelholzzweig
1013 Klavier (Mehrfachbelichtung)
1014 Seetang im Gras, Negativ
1015 Koralle, 10fach vergrößert
1016 Achat, 49fach vergrößert
1017 Tänzerin Hilde Engel
1018 (Fenster)
1019 (Blüte)
1020 Haemanthusstengel
1021 Doppelbildnis
1022 (Porträt mit Monokel)
1023 (Küste)
1024 Buhne
1025 Franz Roh

Photographie als Kunst

1001 ~~xxxKerkex~~ Jaromir Funke, Aus der Serie "Abstraktionen"1927-29
1002 --- " ---
1003 Jindrich Stryski (1894-1942) o.T. (Maske)
1004 Miroslav Hák (1911-1978) Akt
1005 Umbo (1902-1982?) Marga Lion , 1928
1006 Umbo,Pantoffeln, 1928
1007 André Kertesz, Aus der Serie "Distortions" 1933
1008 Berenice Abbott (1898 -) o.T. (Porträt)
1009 Kertesz, Satirische Tänzerin, 1926
1010 Walker Evans (1906-1975) Aus der Serie der FSA - Arbeiten
1011 Kertesz, Marc und Bella Chagall

Dias Fotogeschichte

Die Welt ist schön. Einhundert Photographische Aufnahmen von Albert Renger - Patzsch. Herausgegeben und Eingeleitet von Carl Georg Heise, München 1928

Albert Renger - Patzsch, (1897-1966)

1o26 Sempervivum percarneum

1o27 Sempervivum tabulaeforme

1o28 Agave

1o29 Brasilianischer Melonenbaum

1o3o Mantelpavian

1o31 Natterkopf

1o32 Krabbenfischerin

1o33 Wasserbecken mit Seerosen. Park in Blankenese.

1o34 Gebirgsforst im Winter.

1o35 Schienenweg durch die Sandhaufen einer Zementfabrik. Mathilden - Hütte bei Bad Harzburg.

1o36 Musterzimmer im Fagus-Werk Benscheidt in Alfeld. Schuhleisten - und Stanzmesser-Fabrik.

1o37 Glas

1o38 Kaffee Hag. Plakatentwurf.

1o39 Holzlager der Firma Jost Hinrich Havemann & Sohn, Lübeck

1o4o Turm der Kathol. Hofkirche in Dresden. Perspektivische Ansicht

1o41 Eingangsmauer zum Fagus - Werk Benscheidt in Alfeld. Schuhleisten und Stanzmesser-Fabrik

1o42 Treppe in der Diele eines Privathauses. Architekt Professor Alfred Fischer, Essen

1o43 Vorstadthäuser

1o44 Dampfabstellrad einer 1ooo P.S.-Dampfmaschine. Hannover, Continental-Werke.

1o45 Laufkran im Hochofenwerk Herrenwyck

1o46 Winderhitzer im Hochofenwerk Herrenwyck.

1o47 Laufschiene einer Seilbahn. Mathilden-Höhe bei Bad Harzburg

1o48 Karussell

1o49 Eisbildung an einem Wasserfall

Brücke mit trocknenden Fischernetzen

1o5o Kauper, von unten gesehen. Hochofenwerk. Herrenwyck.

1o51 Bügeleisen für Schuhfabrikation. Fagus-Werk Benscheidt in Alfeld.

1o52 Hände. (Letzte Abbildung im Buch und Ende)

1o53

Dr. Erich Salomon, Berühmte Zeitgenossen in unbewachten Augenblicken. Mit 112 Bildern, J.Engelhorns Nachf. Stuttgart 1931

1o54 Erich Salomon (1886-1944), Gustav Stresemann vor dem Völkerbund, Genf, Sept. 1929

1o55 Aristide Briand, Genf 1929
Nachtsitzung, Haager Konferenz, 11 Uhr und 1 Uhr nachts

1o56 Sir Austen Chamberlain und E. Salomon, London, April 1929

1o57 Verhandlungspause, Paris

1o58 Fridjof Nansen und die engl. Journalistin Miß Round, Genf

1o59 Der kan. Außenminister Dandurand und Dr. Lange, Norwegen

1o6o Arbeitsminister Dr. Stegerwald (li) und Reichsverkehrsminister Dr. von Guérard, Berlin

1o61 Deutsche Diplomaten nach einem Bankett, Berlin

1o62 Der franz. Pazifist Abbé Desgranges, Berlin 1931

1o63 Der Redakteur des "Matin" Jules Sauerwein in einem Kabarett in Wiesbaden

1o64 Eine Sitzung des High Court, London

1o65 Wilhelm Furtwängler dirigiert in der Queen's Hall, London

1o66 Pablo Casals im Odeon in München

1o67 Pablo Casals in der Berliner Philharmonie

1o68 Max Liebermann in seiner Wohnung in Berlin, Mai 1931

1o69 --- d. o. ---

1o7o Dr. Alfred Kerr

1o71 Vater kommt von der Arbeit nach Hause (Selbstbildnis)

1o72 Julien Vallou de Villeneuve, Halbakt mit Wasserkrug, ca 1853 Salzpapierabzug

1o73 Oscar Gustave Rejlander, Akt, Albumin 1857

1o74 Rejlander, Detail aus "Die zwei Wege des Lebens" Gelatine-Silber-Druck, 1974 vom Koll.-Neg. , 1857

1o75 Louis Camille d'Olivier, Aktstudie: Sitzende Frau, Salzpapier?, ca 1854

1o76 F. Jacques Moulin, Aktstudie: Amélie, Salzpapierabzug,ca 1853

1o77 Thomas Eakins, Zwei männl. Akte am Strand, Platindr.,ca 188o

1o78 Wilhelm von Gloeden, Taormina (zwei Knaben) Alb., ca 1899

1o79 René Le Bègue, Academie, Gummidruck mit Ockerpigment und Bleistiftstrichen, 19o2 (Rückenakt)

1o8o Fred Holland Day, Jugendlicher Akt, der sich an einen Felsblock lehnt, Platindruck, 19o7

1o81 Clarence Hudson White und Alfred Stieglitz, Miss Thompson, Gewachster Platindruck, 19o7

1o82 Robert Demachy, Académie, Gummidruck mit Graupigment, 19oo

1o83 Robert Demachy (1859-1938) Académie (Akt) 19oo
Gummidruck mit Graupigment

1o84 F.J. Bellocq, Prostituierte, Storyville, New Orleans,
Neg. 1912, getonter Gel.-Silber-Dr., ca 197o

1o85 Alvin Langdon Coburn, Der Denker (George Bernard Shaw) 19o6
Platin-Gummidruck

1o86 Emil Otto Hoppé (1878-1972) Nijinski in "La Spectre de la
Rose", ca 1916, Platindruck

1o87 Heinrich Kühn (1866-1944) Männl.Akt, ca 191o, Bromöldruck

1o88 Edward Weston (1886-1958) Neil, ca 1925, Platindruck

1o89 Dorothea Lange(1895-1965) Torso (Akt) 1923,

1o9o Edward Weston, Neil, 1925, Platindruck

1o91 Edward Weston, Akt, 1927,

1o92 Rudolf Koppitz (gest.1936,Öst.) Bewegungsstudie, 1926,
Bromöldruck

1o93 Erwin Blumenfeld (1897-1969) Akt unter nassem Seide, 1938

1o94 Francis Brugière (1879-1945) Rosalinde Fuller mit Cello,
ca 193o, Montage

1o95 Lotte Jacobi (1896-) Claire Bauroff, Bln, ca 1928

1o96 Imogen Cunningham, Dreieck (Akt) 1928

1o97 Ray Albert, o.T. (Akt) nach 193o, getönter Gel.Silber-Dr.

1o98 Edward Weston, Akt, Oceano, Kalifornien, 193o

1o99 George Platt-Lynes (19o7-1955) o.T. (männl. Akt) nach 193o
Doppelbelichtung

11oo Platt-Lynes, Salvador Dali, 1939

11o1 Erwin Blumenfeld, o.T. (Akt) 194o

11o2 Platt-Lynes, o.T. (Akt) 1941

11o3 Platt-Lynes, Douglas Coudy und Lew Christensen in Balanchines
"Orpheus", 1938

Katalog Photographie als Kunst

11o4 Dorothea Lange, Aus der Serie der FSA - Arbeiten

11o5 Lange, FSA

11o6 Ben Shan (1898-1969) o.T. (FSA)

11o7 Jack Delano, o.T. (FSA)

11o8 Paul Strand (189o-1976) Aus dem Portfolio "On my doorstep"

11o9 Strand, Aus dem Portfolio "On my doorstep"

Dias Fotogeschichte

111o Felix H. Man (Hans Baumann) (1893-1983) Benito Mussolini in seinem Arbeitszimmer in Rom, 1931

1111 Alfred Eisenstaedt (1898 -)Ballettänzer bei einer Pause

1112 Robert Frank (1924), Flohmarkt, 1964

1113 Bill Brandt (19o4-), Porträt eines jungen Mädchens, Eaton Place

1114 Yousuf Karsh, Sir Winston Churchill, 1941

1115 Lucien Clergue (1934), Aus "Nus de la Mer" ab 1956

1116 Lucien Clergue, Aus "Nus de la Mer" ab 1956

1117 Josef Sudek (1896-1976) o.T. (Stilleben mit Akt)

1118 Sudek, Stilleben

1119 Christian Staub (1918- Schweiz, jetzt USA) o.T.(Konservenbüchsenstilleben)

112o Sudek, o.T. (Stilleben)

Andreas Haus, Raoul Hausmann, Kamerafotografien 1927-1957,
München 1979

1121 Raoul Hausmann (1886-1971) "The reporter" 1931
1122 Schreibmaschine und Frauennacken, ca 1931, Doppelbelicht.
1123 Berlin, S-Bahnhof Charlottenburg, 1930-31
1124 Berlin 1930-31
1125 Porträt Schmidt-Rottluff, 1930
1126 Blick in den Rasierspiegel, 1930-31
1127 Frauenbildnis, nach 1930
1128 Porträt Christa Ranitsch, (Le Rêve) 1930
1129 Selbstbildnis, Ostsee 1931
1130 Strandbild Ostsee 1931 (Porträt-Akt)
1131 Strandbild 1931
1132 Akt, Ostsee, 1931 (?)
1133 Akt , Ostsee, 1931
1134 Akt Ostsee, ca 1930
1135 Akte, Ostsee ca 1930
1136 Akt, Ostsee, 1930/31
1137 Akt, Ostsee, 1930/31
1138 Akt, Ostsee, ca 1931
1139 Akt, Ostsee (Mouvement II) 1931, enger Ausschnitt aus Querformat
1140 Brust und Hand, ca 1930
1141 Akt bei der Toilette, ca 1930
1142 Frauennacken, ca 1930, Kunstlichtaufnahme
1143 Rückeakt, ca 1930, Kunstlicht
1144 Schatten einer Stuhllehne auf weißem Karton, vor 1931 Kunstlichtaufn.
1145 o.T., o.D. (Licht und Schatten)
1146 Lichtmühle (Papierkorb von innen beleuchtet (1931)
1147 Lichtmühle, 1931
1148 Lichtmühle, 1931
1149 Toilettengegenstände, Handschuh, ca 1930
1150 Kasserollen, Limoges, ca 1950, enger Ausschn., Neg. 9 x 12
1151 Stuhl und Melone, Ibiza, 1935
1152 Chrysantheme, ca 1930

Das Selbstporträt im Zeitalter der Photographie. Maler und Photographen im Dialog mit sich selbst. Herausgegeben von Erika Billeter mit einem Vorwort von Michel Tournier de l'Académie Goncourt, Württembergischer Kunstverein Stuttgart, Musée cantonal des Beaux-Arts Lausanne 1985

1171 Eugène Delacroix, 1842, Selbstporträt, ausgeführt von Riesener, Daguerreotypie, Original verloren

1172 Adrien Tournachon um 1855, Selbstporträt
73 Fred Boissonas, 1891, Selbstporträt
74 Ilse Bing, Selbstporträt 1931
75 Michel Seuphor, Selbstporträt 1929
76 André Kertesz, Selbstporträt 1976
77 Gertrude Käsebier, Selbstporträt um 1900
78 Ilse Bing, 1931
79 Lotte Jacobi um 1930
1180 André Kertész bei Aufnahmen von "Distorsions" 1922
81 Weegee 1942
82 Jacques Henri Lartigue 1920, Umbo um 1929, Raoul Hausmann 1919 mit Hannah Höch
83 Man Ray und Paul Eluard, 1940
84 Félix Nadar in indianischem Köstüm für einen Maskenball, 1863
1153 O.G.Rejlander um 1860 (alle 4 Fotografien)
1154 Louis Ducos du Hauron, 1889, anamorphotische Porträts
1155 Fred Holland Day, die letzten sieben Tage Christi, 1898 um
56 Wilhelm von Gloeden, Selbstporträt 1900, Frine ed Figli, 1914
57 Egon Schiele, Posenfoto in Zusammenarbeit mit Anton Trcka, 1914/1
58 George Hoyningen-Huene, Selbstporträt
59 Alfred Eisenstaedt, 1976, Selbstportr.Überlagerung v.Neg.en
1160 Félix Nadar, um 1854
61 Félix Nadar, zwischen 1865 - 1889
62 Eugène Disderi um 1860
63 Pierre Petit, 1863, Selbstporträt, Studie, auf einem Stuhl schlafend, (1832 - nach 1900)
64 Imogen Cunningham, um 1910
65 Imogen Cunningham um 1913, 1933, 1958
66 Imogen Cunningham, 1974
67 J. H. Lartigue, 1919, Selbstporträt als Maler
68 Florence Henri, 1938
69 Man Ray, 1940 und Juliet
1170 Man Ray, 1943

Ernst Fuhrmann, Die Pflanze als Lebewesen. Eine Biographie in 2oo Aufnahmen, 193o, Societäts-Verlag, Frankfurt am Main

1185 Ernst Fuhrmann (1886-1956) Pinie, 193o
1186 Gartenerbse, Keimlinge
1187 Rhabarber, Knospe
1188 Art der Aloe
1189 Kürbis, Ranke
119o Kürbis, Ranke
1191 Zantedeschie
1192 Zaunrebe
1193 Wiesenbocksart. Flugschirme oben fehlend
1194 Berg-Ulme. Halberverweste Samen
1195 Reiherschnabel. Same. Reif
1196 Besenstrauch
1197 Schwertlilie. Weiblicher Blütenteil
1198 Fichte. Männliche Blüte
1199 Helmknabenkraut
1200 Knabenkraut-Variation
12o1 Vogelnestwurz
12o2 Pappelgallen
12o3 Exotische Efeuart
12o4 Disteltrieb

Erika Billeter, Amerika Fotografie 192o-194o, Hannover 198o

12o5 James Abbe, Adolf Hitler, Jan. 1932
12o6 James Abbe, Joseph Paul Goebbels, 1933
12o7 James Abbe, Hermann Göring, 1933
12o8 Jack Delano (1914-) Negerfrau, Greene County, Georg.,1941
12o9 Delano, Alte Leute, Greene County, Georgia, 1941
121o Aaron Siskind, (19o3-) Kopf eines Negerjungen, 1933
1211 Imogen Cunningham, Gertrude Stein, 1937
1212 Cunningham, Edward Weston und Margrethe, 1923
1213 Alfred Stieglitz, Equivalent, 1923
1214 Stieglitz, Mountain in Sky, 1924
1215 A.L. Coburn, (1883-1966) Vortograph, 1917
1216 Francis Brugière (1882-1945) o.T. (exper. Fotografie)
1217 Brugière, Weggang in verächtlichem Elend, ca 1929
1218 George Platt-Lynes, Max Ernst, 1941
1219 Platt-Lynes, George Grosz

1220 Werner Gräff, Es kommt der neue Fotograf, Berlin 1929 Umschlag

1221 Gräff

1222 Gräff, Hubacher

1223 Gräff, Hubacher, Giedion

1224 Gräff, Gräff

1225 Gräff, Werthoff, Gräff

1226 Gräff

1227 Gräff, Sasha Stone

1228 Gräff

1229 Gräff

1230 Gräff, Gräff

1231 Gräff, W. Baumeister

1232 Gräff, Herbert Bayer

Beaumont Newhall, The history of photography, New York 1982

1233 Paul Strand (1890-1976) (Maschinendetail) 1922

1234 A.L.Coburn, Haus der tausend Fenster, New York, 1912

1235 Dorothea Lange, Umherziehende Mutter, Nipomo, Californien 1938

1236 Alfred Stieglitz, New York - Nachts, 1931

1237 Paul Strand, Porträt Washington-Square, New York, 1916 aus: Camera Work, 1917, Photogravure

1238 Paul Strand, Gestein, Porte Lone, Nova Scotia o.J.

1239 Paul Strand, Stadthaus, Vermont, 1946

1240 Charles Sheeler (1883-1965) Ford-Werk, Detroit, 1927

1241 Edward Weston, Wolken-Mexiko, 1926, Akt, 1925, Platindruck

1242 Walker Evans (1903-1975) Alice Mae Burroughs, Frau eines Baumwollpächters, Alabama 1936

1243 Lisette Model, Promenade des Anglais, 1937

1244 Oskar Barnack, Ernst Leitz, 1917

1245 Moholy-Nagy, Eifersucht, 1927, Fotomontage

1246 Moholy-Nagy, Leda und der Schwan, 1925, Fotomontage

1247 Antonio Gulio Bragaglia (1890-1960) Grüße!, 1911, Der futuristische Maler Giacomo Balla, 1912

1248 Erich Mendelsohn, Equitable Trust Building, New York, aus: (1924) Amerika-Bilderbuch eines Architekten, Berlin 1928

1249 A.L. Coburn, Haus der 1000 Fenster, New York, 1912

Erika Billeter, Amerika-Fotografie 1920-1940

1250 James Abbe, Nuremburg-Rennen, im Vordergrund Sturm- Truppen 1933

Dias Fotogeschichte

Kat. Werner Mantz. Architekturphotographie in Köln 1926-1932 aus der Graphischen Sammlung des Museums Ludwig der Stadt Köln, Köln 1982, Ber.bib. Kuwi

1251 Werner Mantz (19o1-)Wohnhaus in Köln,Gyrhofstr.2o,ca 1928
1252 Köln, Siedlungsbauten am Geraer Platz, 1928
1253 Köln, Siedlung Bickendorf, ca 1929
1254 Siedlung Köln-Kelkerfeld,Heidelberger Str. ca 193o
1255 Köln-Ehrenfeld, Alpenerstr., 1927
1256 Köln, Haus Kops, Hofansicht, 193o
1257 Köln, Haus Georgii, Westseite, 1928
1258 Treppenhaus des Hauses Dr. G., Köln, 1927
1259 Köln, Treppenhaus des Ursulinen-Lyzeums,Georgenplatz, 193o

Jean-Hubert Martin (Hrg.) Man Ray.Photographs, London1982, Ber.bib.Kuwi

126o Man Ray, Nusch Eluard, Ady
1261 o.T., Meret Oppenheim
1262 Nusch Eluard, Sonja Mosse, 1936
1263 o.T. (Akt) 1925
1264 Nusch Eluard, 1935
1265 Rétour à la raison, 1923 (Akt)
1266 Kiki de Montparnasse, 1922
1267 Noire et blanche, 1926
1268 o.T., Meret Oppenheim, 1933
1269 o.T.)männl. Akt)
127o Selbstporträt
1271 Selbstporträts
1272 Selbstporträt
1273 Rayographie, 1922
1274 Rayographie, 1926
1275 Rayographie
1276 Rayographie 1927
1277 Perspective d'un cube d'une sphère, d'une cône et d'un cylindre, 1937 /36
1278 L'aurore des objets, 1937
1279 Ombre II 1934
128o Integration of shadows 1919
1281 o.T. (Pflanze)
1282 o.T. (Pflanze)
1283 Lee Miller, ca 193o
1284 Barbette, 1926

1285 Man Ray, Virginia Woolf, 1933
1286 Gertrude Stein, 1926
1287 Coco Chanel, ca 1935
1288 Modefotografien, 1925
1289 La Femme, 1926
1290 Rrose Sélavy, 1921
1291 Tonsure, 1921
1292 Ciné-sketch: Adam, Eve: Marcel Duchamp, Brogna Perlmutter-Clair, 1924
1293 Kurt Schwitters, 1936
1294 Meret Oppenheim, 1933
1295 Max Ernst, ca 1935 Solarisation
1296 Palais de quatre heures, 1932-33
1297 Luis Bunuel, 1929
1298 Yves Tanguy, 1936

Erika Billeter (Hrg) Malerei und Photographie im Dialog von 184o bis heute. Mit Beiträgen von Prof.J.A. Schmoll gen.Eisenwerth 1977/79 Zürich und Bern

1299 Marconi, Modellfotos (Akt)

1300 Aufnahme eines afrikan. Königs i.ei.Reiseroman von Emil Ludwig "Die Reise nach Afrika", 1913 und Oskar Schlemmer, König Daudi, Aquarell um 1913

1301 Max Ernst, Der Kaiser von Wahana, Öl auf Leinwand, um 192o

1302 Franz von Lenbach, Fot.e Bildnisstudie zum Gemälde, 19o3 mit Selbstauslöser, Bildnisstudie mit Frau und Töchtern, Öl auf Pappe, 19o3

1303 Franz von Stuck, Skizze zum Gemälde "Franz v.St. u.Gattin im Atelier, Bildnis der Gattin Mary,Foto, Selbstporträt vor Staffelei, Foto, Gemälde, Öl auf Leinwand 19o2

1304 An., Porträtstudie von Jane Morris im Auftrag von Dante Gabriel Rossetti, 1865

1305 An., Jane Morris, Nr. 12o von Rossetti als Vorlage zum Bild "Rêverie" benutzt

1306 An., Jane Morris

1307 Franz von Lenbach, Otto Fürst von Bismarck

1308 Franz v.Lenbach, Bismarck im Sessel, Öl auf Leinwand, 1895 Bildnisstudien B.s, insgs. exist. über 1oo

1309 Louis Jacques Mandé Daguerre, Personnages visitant une ruine médiévale, Öl auf Leinwand, 1826

1310 Edgar Degas, Mallarmé und Renoir auf dem Divan
1311 Thomas Eakins, Walt Whiman, ca 1891 (während Arbeit zum Gemälde
1312 Henry Peach Robinson, When the Day's work is done, Alb., 1877
1313 Robert Demachy, Dans les sapins, Neg. vor 19o6, mit Öl überarb.
1314 Constant Puyo, Sommer

Dias Fotogeschichte

Newhall, History of Photography

1315 An., Académie, ca 1845, Dag.
1316 Antoine Claudet, Familiengruppe, ca 1852, Stereodag.
1317 Henri Le Secq, Treppenturm, Rue de la Petite Boucherie,
1318 Chartres
Charles Nègre, Ölmühlen in Grasse, 1852, Cal. neg.
1319 Hippolyte Bayard, Die Madeleine, ca 1845 (Wandelgang)
~~1320~~

Jerry L Thompson, Walker Evans at Work, London 1983, VBK-Bib.

1320 Paul Grotz, Walker Evans bei der Arbeit, 1929
1321 New York City, 1928-29, "Broadway Composition"
1322 Coney Island, New York 1928/29
1323 Provinzstadt, 1931
1324 Victorianische Architektur, 1930-31
1325 (Form)
1326 Cuba 1932 (Porträt)
1327 Cuba 1932 (Porträt)
1328 Alabama 1936 "
1329 Alabama 1936 "
1330 South Carolina (Arch)

Gisèle Freund, Memoiren des Auges, Frankfurt a.M. 1977 VBK-Bib.

1331 Gisèle Freund, Nazi-Studenten in Frankfurt a.M., 1932
1332 Walter Benjamin, Paris 1939
1333 Stefan Zweig, London 1939
1334 Samuel Beckett (Warten auf Godot) Paris 1964
1335 Schaufenster eines Friseursalons-Paris 1935
1336 Virginia Woolf, London 1939
1337 André Gide unter der Maske von Leopardi, in seiner Wohnung in Paris, 1939
1338 Adrienne Monnier, Buchhändlerin und Herausgeberin, Paris 1939
1339 James Joyce, Paris 1939
1340 Jean-Paul Sartre , Paris 1939
1341 Simone de Beauvoir, Paris 1939
1342 André Malraux, Paris 1939
1343 Henri Matisse, La Cannet 1947
1344 Jean Cocteau, Paris 1939

Katalog Aktfotografie, München 1985

1345 An., Stereodaguerreotypie, ca 1855 + Hälfte einer an. Stereo-dag. ca 1855 (Rückenakte
1346 Hälfte einer an.Stereodag.,ca 1855 Perseus und Andromache
1347 John Hilliard, Naked, 1981
1348 David Hockney, Brian, 1982
1349 Wilhelm Loth, Akt, 1982
1350 Les Krims, A Marxist View, 1984
1351 Lucas Samaras, Aus der Serie 20-24, 1980
1352
1353 Guy Bourdin für Vogue Francais, Ariel 1979

Erika Billeter, Amerika Fotografie 1920-40, Hannover 1980, Stabi

1354 Weegee (Arthur Fellig) (1899-1968), Schlafende Kinder auf einer Feuertreppe, 1938
1355 Weegee, Ertrunkener, Coney Island, ca 1940
1356 Weegee, Ostersonntag in Harlem, 1940
1357 Weegee, Wohnungsbrand, Harlem 1942
1358 Lisette Model (1906-) Frau in Coney Island, ca 1944
1359 Model, Sänger in Sammy's Bowery (Ausschnitt)
1360 Model, Frau mit Schal, East Side, New York, ca 1940
1361 Model, ---" ---

Laszlo Glozer, Wols Photograph, Hannover 1978, Stabi

1362 Paris
1363 Paris
1364 Paris
1365 Paris
1366 Paris
1367 Cassis

Dias Fotogeschichte

1368 Wols, Paris
1369 Paris
1370 Paris
1371 Paris
1372 Cassis
1373 Nicole Boubant
1374 Jacques Prévert und Jacqueline Laurent
1375 Roger Gilbert -Lecomte
1376 Gréty Wols
1377 Selbstporträt
1378 Jean Sendy (Abelson)
1379 Germaine Demeure (Akt)
1380 o.T. (Mund)
1381 Addy Martiniquaise (Halbakt)
1382 o.T. (Rückenakt)
1383 o.T. (Stilleben)
1384 o.T. (Rinnstein)
1385 o.T. (Zuckerstücke)
1386 o.T. (Schoten?)
1387 o.T. (Zwiebel)
1388 o.T. (Fleischstück)
1389 o.T. (abgehäuteter Tierkopf)
1390 o.T. (abgehäuteter Hase)
1391 o.T. (Stilleben mit Tierteilen)
1392 o.T. (Fotoatelier
1393 o.T. (Nieren?)

Graham Howe, G. Ray Hawkins (Ed.s): Paul Outerbridge Jr. Photographs 1921-39 , London 1980, Stabi

1394 Ide Collar 1922
1395 "Fantaisie" 1926 (Stilleben)
1396 HO-Box 1922
1397 Triumph des Eis, 1932
1398 Modell 1923
1399 Akt im Sessel 1923
1400 Ethiopian Form 1923 (männl. Halbakt)

1401 Paul Outerbridge, Krug und Tortenbleche, 1923
1402 Mannequin, 1927
1403 Butterfly Abstraction, ca 1929
1404 Beine in Strümpfen mit Blumen, 1928

Evemlyn Weiss (Hrg.), Alexander Rodtschenko. Fotografien 1920-1938, Köln 1978, Stabi

1405 M.A. Kaufmann, Porträtfoto Alexander Rodtschenko (1891-1956) 1921
1406 Alexander Rodtschenko, Titelseite zu Pro Eto, 1923
1407 Pro Eto. 1923
1408 Pro Eto, 1923
1409 Pro Eto, 1923
1410 Kiefer (Puschkino - Wald) 1925
1411 Balkone, 1926
1412 Mädchen mit Leica, 1934
1413 Mädchenkopf, 1930
1414 Telefonierende Frau (W. Stepanowa) 1923
1415 W. Stepanowa, 1928
1416 Satejniki-Park für Kultur und Freizeit, Moskau, ca 1927
1417 Ossip Brik, 1924
1418 Porträt der Mutter, 1924
1419 Majakowsky, 1924
1420 A. Schewtschenko, 1924
1421 W(arwara) Stepanowa, 1925
1422 Pionier-Mädchen
1423 Pionier mit Horn, 1930
1424 Innenhof, 1927
1425 Straße in Moskau, ca 1920
1426 Bolschoi-Theater, Moskau, ca 1932
1427 Akrobatin, 1937
1428 Im Zirkus, 1937
1429 Im Zirkus, 1937
1430 Der Sprung ins Wasser (Kunstspringer) 1935
1431 Fesselballon
1432 Auf dem Barren, 1938
1433 Sportverein Dynamo, 1930

Nicolas Ducrot (Ed.) André Kertész. Distortions, London 1977
ZBB d VBK

1434 André Kertész, Distortions, Akte ohne bes. Titel, 1. Hälfte der 3oer Jahre

1435 "-"-

1436 -"-

1437 -"-

1438 -"-

1439 -"-

144o -"-

1441 -"-

1442 -"-

1443 -"-

1444 -"-

1445 -"-

1446 -"-

~~144~~

Christian Brandstätter (Hrg.), Lothar Rübelt. Österreich zwischen den Kriegen. Zeitdokumente eines Photopioniers der 2oer und 3oer Jahre, Wien, München, Zürich o.J. (1985) Stabi

1447 Lothar Rübelt, Winterliche Straßenszene in der Wiener Mariahilfer Straße,2oer

1448 Hundekorso auf der Wiener Ringstraße März 1929
Werbung für den Tag des Buches am 22.3.1929 durch Pfadfinder vor der Wiener Oper

1449 Demonstrationsfahrt der Wiener Taxis auf dem Stephansplatz, Jan. 1933

145o Beseitigung von Sturmschäden an einer Leitung

1451 Gepäcksträger vor dem Franz-Joseph-Bahnhof, 1929

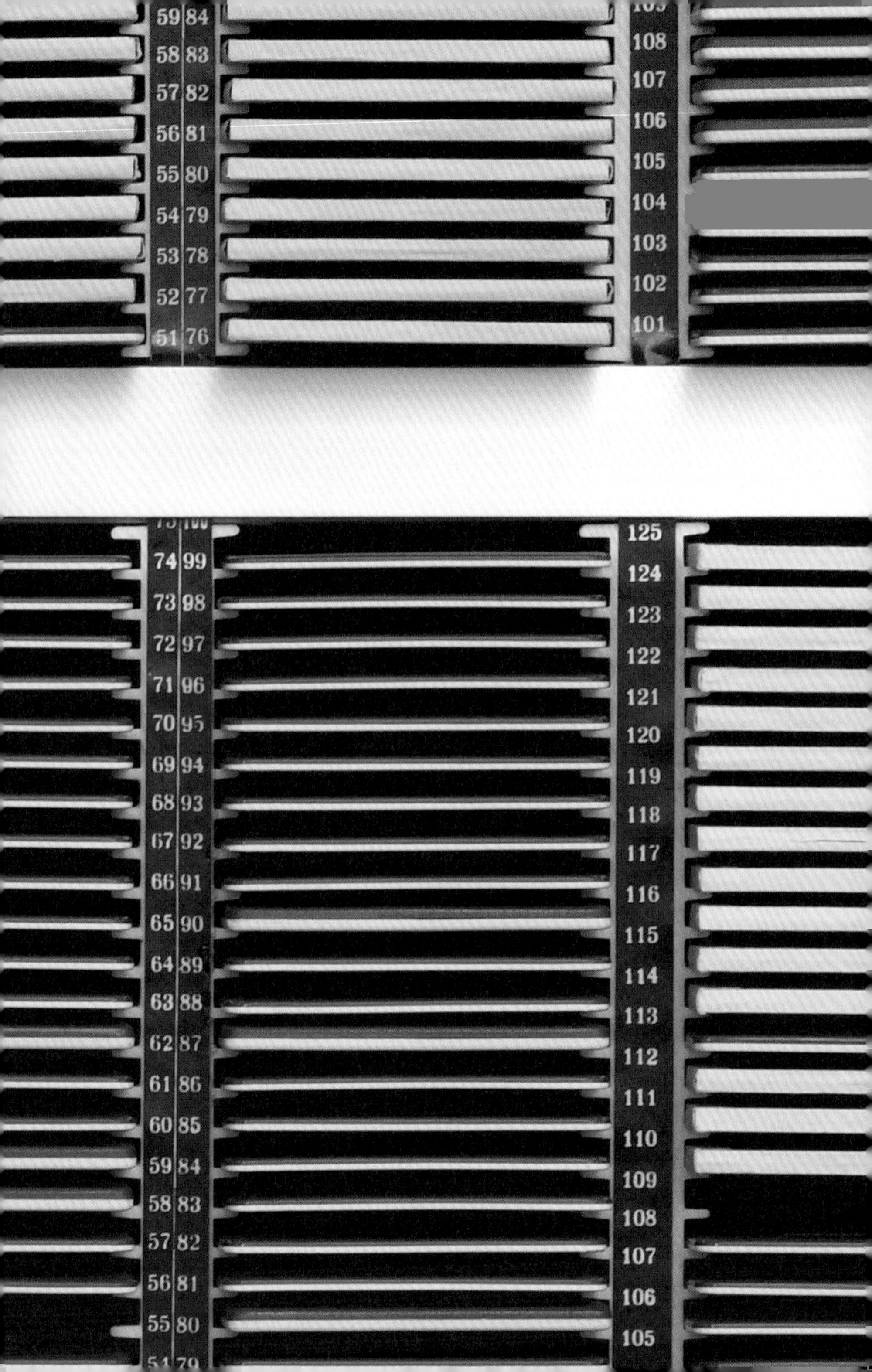
59 84
58 83 108
57 82 107
56 81 106
55 80 105
54 79 104
53 78 103
52 77 102
51 76 101
125
74 99 124
73 98 123
72 97 122
71 96 121
70 95 120
69 94 119
68 93 118
67 92 117
66 91 116
65 90 115
64 89 114
63 88 113
62 87 112
61 86 111
60 85 110
59 84 109
58 83 108
57 82 107
56 81 106
55 80 105

Rainer Fabian, Hans Christian Adam, Masters of Early Travel Photography, London 1983, ZI f Kuwi

1452 Francis Frith, Die Kolossal-Statue Ramses II. In Theben, 1857
1453 Frith, Kolosse in der Nubischen Wüste, 1857
1454 Frith, Kalifengräber bei Kairo, ca 1857
1455 Frith, Tempel auf der Insel Philae, 1857, i.Vordergrund Boot des Fotografen
1456 Maxime Du Camp, Statue von Ramses dem Großen in Abu Simbel, 1850
1457 Frith, Bas-Relief im Großen Tempel in Philae, 1857
1458 Frith, Löwen -Kopf an der Außenwand des Tempels v.Dendera,1857
1459 Dunmore u.Critcherson, Eiseberge im Baffin's Bay, 1869
1460 Dunmore u.Critcherson, William Bradford u.s.Begleiter, 1869
1461 Baron Stillfried(?), Doppel-Porträt, ca 1880
1462 Felice Beato, Japan Offizier, ca 1875
1463 An., Japan. Gruß-Zeremonie, ca 1885
1464 Kusakabe(?)Kimbei, Geisha mit abgewendetem Rücken, ca 1880
1465 Baron Stillfried, Regen-Schauer im Studio (Genrebild) ca 1875
1466 Kusakabe Kimbei, Feuerwehrleute beim Neujahrsfestival, ca 1890
1467 Baron Stillfried(?)Artistenkind mit Feder-Kopfschmuck, ca 1880
1468 An., Menschliche Pyramide, ca 1890
1469 An., Tätowierter, ca 1880
1470 Baron Stillfried(?), Samurais vor gemaltem Hintergrund, ca 1880
1471 Bourne u.Shepherd(?)Der Maharadscha von Rewah, ca 1877
1472 Samuel Bourne, Tor zum Markt von Lucknow, 1865
1473
1474 Bourne, Pilgerstraße in Srinagar, 1864
1475 Bourne, Inneres der Moschee von Agra, 1865
1476 Bourne, Ureinwohner in der Bergen von Südindien, ca 1863
1477 Bourne, Pfad im Himalaya, 1866
1478 John Thomson, Umwickelte Füße von Chines. Frauen, ca 1870
1479 Thomson, Einer von der Straßenwache, 1871
1480 Thomson, Kolor.Porträt eines Chinesenmädchens, ca 1868
1481 Thomson, Ches. Dame der höheren Gesellschaft, ca 1868
1482 Thomson, Chines. Kohlengräber, ca 1870
1483 Thomson, Bettlerkönig mit drei seiner Leute in der Hafenstadt Fuchow, ca 1870
1484 Thomson, Betagte Dame (Typen der arbeitenden Klassen) 1870
1485 Thomson, Chines. Kuli,
1486 Marc Ferrez, Wasserfall von Paquequer, ca 1878
1487 Ferrez, Indianer des Botocudo-Stammes in der Prov. Bahia, 1875
1488 Ferrez, Häuptling Cumbo de Ucayala (At.aufnahme) 1875

Graham Howe, G. Ray Hawkins (Ed.)
Paul Outerbridge Jr.: Photographs 1921-39, London 1980, Stabi
color

1489 Outerbridge, Akt mit Rahmen, 1938
1490 Akt mit Maske
1491 Akt im Bad
1492 liegender Akt
1493 Glas und Koralle
1494 Akt mit Handtuch, ca 1937
1495 Akt mit Katze, ca 1939
1496 Maskierter Akt mit Hut, ca 1936
1497 Sitzender Akt, ca 1937
1498 "Images de Deauville" ca 1936
1499 Mannequin mit Hautkrem, ca 1936
1500 Frau mit Krallen, 1937
1501 Aufsteigender Phoenix, ca 1937
1502 Torso, ca 1936
1503 Hände mit Maske, ca 1934
1504 Maske, Kegel und Muscheln, ca 1937
1505 Liegender Akt, ca 1936
1506 Akt mit Maske und Hut, ca 1936

Fotografien aus der Collection Stübel
Forscherarchiv des Instituts für Geographie und Geoökologie der AdW, Leipzig

---

+ Carte de Visite

1507 1 Indianerin mit Kropf, Gegend von Popayan, Colombia 1868 +

1508 2 Indianer von Cotacachi, Ecuador 1870-74 +

1509 3 Indianer von Otavalo, -- " -- +

1510 4 Indianer von Zambiza bei Quito, -- " -- +

1511 5 Indianer von La Magdalena, -- " -- +

1512 6 Indianerin von Zambiza, -- " -- +

1513 7 Indianerin von La Magdalena, -- " -- +

1514 8 Indianer der Gegend von La Paz, Pongo, Bolivien 1876 +

1515 9 "Aus der Umgebung des Titicacasees", "in Arequipa gekauft" Bolivien 1876 +

1516 10 ---- " ---- +

1517 11 Gegend von La Paz, Peon, in A. gekauft, Bol. 1876 +

1518 12 ---- " ---- (identisch)

1519 13 Umgebung des Titicacasees, Aymara-Indianer, in A. gek. Bol. 1876 +

1519 13 Indianer von Ancoraimes, Bol. 1876 +

1520 14 Indianer von Ancoraimes am Titicacasee, Hochland von Bol. 1876 +

1521 15 Seminarist mit Indianerknaben. La Paz, In A. gekauft Hochland von Bolivien, 1876 +

1522 16 Indianerin von Potosi, Hochland von Bol., 1876 +

1523 17 Indianer von Potosi, Hochland von Bol., 1876 +

1524 18 Neger-Typen. Sklavinnen, z.T. noch in Afrika geboren, Alberto Henschel & Co., Pernambuco, Brasilien 1875, Pernambuco +

1525 19 -- " -- +

1526 20 -- " -- +

1527 21 -- " -- +

1528 22 -- " -- , Bahia (Halbakt) +

1529 23 --, " -- , Pernambuco +

1530 24 Neger Typen. Sklaven, ... , Bahia +

1531 25 -- " -- +

1532 26 -- " -- +

1533 27 Arara. Indianerin von Rio Negro. Vom Photographen aufgeputzt. F.A. Fidanza, Pará, Brasilien 1875, Rio Amazonas +

Collection Stübel

1534 28 El Coronel Vilca.(Huilea) war der Anführer der Indianer, mit deren Hilfe Morales und Coral den Präsidenten Melgarejo zu stürzen suchten. 2 Jahre später wurde Morales von La Faye, seinem Neffen, erstochen, Vilca von den Indianern vergiftet, in Arequipa gekauft +

1535 29 El Coronel Vilca +

1536 30 Rayo. Der Mörder des Präsidenten G.G. Moreno, E. Courret, Lima, Ecuador

1537 31 G.G. Moreno nach seiner Ermoderung auf der Plaza von Quito, August 1875, Ecuador

1538 32 G.G. Moreno mit den Jesuiten von Quito, Ecuador

1539 33 Die Revolution des 15. Jan. 1871 in La Paz, Bol, 1876

1540 34 Straße in La Paz nach der Revolution von 1871. Barricade N° 8, Bol. 1876

1541 35 La Revolucion de Cochabamba in 1874,. Die Photographie hat der General Daza zur Verherrlichung seiner Person aufnehmen lassen, nachdem der Straßenkampf beendet war.

1542 36 "Callaquallas". Callaqualla von Caquiaviri. In La Paz photographiert. Bolivianische Aerzte und Verkäufer von Heilmitteln. Sie durchwandern ganz Südamerika bis nach Panama, ihre eigentliche Heimt soll das Dorf Caquiaviri sein. Hochland von Bolivien 1876

1543 37 Indios Araucanos, Photographia Universal, Valparaiso, "In Valparaiso gekauft", Chile 1876, Cabinet

1544 38 Cacique Araucano, Chile 1876, Cabinet

1545 39 "Buenas Mozas de Montevideo" Frauen-Typen spanischer Abkunft in Montevideo, Bate & Ca., Montevideo, Uruguay 1876, Cabinet

1546 40 "Buenas Mozas....", Chute & Brooks, Montevideo, Ur. 1876

1547 41 "Buenas Mozas....", Chute & Brooks,

1548 42 Gaucho, Cabinet, Uruguay

1549 43 Die medizinische Fakultät von La Paz, Bolivien 1876

1550 44 Lima. Die Brüder Gutierrez, die Mörder des Präsidenten Balta, vom Volke gelyncht, 1872, Perú +

1551 45 Indianer von Cerro de Pasco, Lima 1877

1552 46 Perusnischer Soldat mit seiner Frau ("Rabona".Die Rabonas begleiten die Soldaten auf Feldzügen, whrsch.Eugenio Manoury, Perú 1876

1553 47 ---- " ----

1554 48 "Rabona" (Stillende) Hermanos Courret, Lima, Perú 1876, +

1555 49 Negrita de Lima, R. Castillo, Lima, Perú 1876 +

1555 49 Negrita de Lima, R. Castillo, Lima, Perû 1876 +

1556 5o Indianer von Cuzco, Hochland von Perù

1557 51 Indianerin, Küstenland von Perù

1558 52 Indianerin, Lima 1877 (Stillende) Küstenland v. Perù

1559 53 La Paz. Oberseite der Plaza Casa de Obispo, Loreto-Kirche und Blick auf den Illimani. Durch das Eckfenster der Casa de Obispo ließ der Präsident Melgarejo auf sein Commando eine Abtheilung Soldaten springen, um ihren militärischen Gehorsam zu prüfen; mehrere Soldaten verunglückten. Die Häuser zeigen noch die Löcher, welche Flintenkugeln in der Revolution von 1871 geschlagen haben.

1560 54 Sucre. Die große Pfingstmesse, La Feria de Resureccion, Bolivien 1876

1561 55 "La China" Bildsäuoe aus rothem Sandstein. Governador militar de Tiahuanaco, Monsieur Ber, ein Verwüster von Althertümern unter dem Vorwande wissenschaftlicher Forschung, Cura de Tiahuanaco, v. Grumbkow phot. 1876 Boliv. 1877, Tiahuanaco

1562 56 El Rio Desaquadero (Abfluß des Titicacasees mit der schwimmenden Brücke. Grenze zwischen Perù und Boliv. Bol./Perù 1877

1563 57 "Medicos bilivianos" Caporales.Aerztlich Ratgeber und Verkäufer von Heilmitteln, Lima 1877, Hochl. von Boliv.

1564 58 Indianische Verbrecher. Strassenräuber vom Wege nach Yungas 1874 (?) gefangen und hingerichtet worden. La Paz Hochland von Boliv. 1876

1565 59 Indianische Verbrecher, La Paz, Hochland v. Boliv.

1566 6o Die Erbauer der Eisenbahn von Còrdoba nach Tucuman Argentinien 1876

1567 61 Die Minen von Chimberro bei Copiapò, Chile 1876

1568 62 Quinta Meiggs Henrx Meiggs Erbauer der Eisenbahnen in Chile und Perù, Chile 1876

1569 63 Quilota. An der Eisenbahn von Valparaiso nach Santiago, Chile 1876

157o 64 Der Hafen von Lota. Steinkohlenwerke, Südchile 1876

1571 65 Rio de Janeiro. Botanischer Garten. Palmen 4o Jahre alt Bras. 1875

1572 66 Rio de Janeiro. Park, Bras. 1875 (Botanik)

1573 67 Bahia. Einfahrt in den Hafen, Bras. 1875

1574 68 Rio San Vicente, A. Frisch, Rio Amazonas, Bras.

1575 69 Cafusa (?), Spinnerin am Rio Negro, Bras. u. Perù

1576 7o Miranha-Indianerinnen, A. Frisch, Rio Amazonas, Bras.1875

1577 71 Amahuas-Indianer. Wohnen am Rio Japura 35 Meilen aufwärts von seiner Mündung in den Rio Amazonas. A. Frisch, Rio Amazonas Bras. 1875

1578 72 Amahuas-Indianer am Rio Japurà, A. Frisch,Rio Amazonas, Bras. 1875

1579 73 Ticuna-Indianer am Rio Calderao, Rio Amazonas,Bras.1875

158o	74	Puerto Cabello "In Panama gekauft" (Dorfstraße mit Riesenkaktus), Venezuela 1877
1581	75	Smaragd-Minen von Muzo, Los Perones, Colombia 1868
1582	76	Oroya-Eisenbahn, Perù 1875 (E.-brücke)
1583	77	Chola. Mischrase, Arequipa ? (Frau vor Gebüsch mit hervorragendem Männerkopf), Hochland von Perù 1876
1584	78	Puno-Arequipa-Eisenbahn. Station Vincocaya (4479 m) nahe dem höchsten Punkte (4543 m) der Bahn, Hochland von Perù 1877
1585	79	La Calichera Argentina (Salpeterwerk) 1o21 m.ü.d.M Nord-Chile 1876
1586	8o	Ruinenstätte von Pumapungu, gegen NO gesehen, Tiahuanaco, v. Grumbkow phot. 1876, Bol. 1877
1587	81	Puno-Arequipa-Eisenbahn: Terraplen de Guisco, Perù 1877
1588	82	-- " --: Aufstieg am Vulcangebirge Charchani,Perù 1877
1587	83	Corocoro. Die Kupferwerke am Fuße des Cerro de Corocoro Boliv. 1876
1588	84	El Vapor "Jo" auf dem Titicacasee (Später Yapurá benannt) Hochland von Perù und Bolivien 1877
1589	85	Cruz de Reaes. Valparaiso, Fotografia E. Garreaud 1878, Chile 1876
159o	86	d. o.
1591	87	Wäscherinnen am Rio de la Plata bei Buenos Aires, Arg. 1876
1591	88	Puenta-Arenas, Magalhaes-Str., Süd-Chile 1876
1592	89	(Am Titicacasee) Hochland von Bol. und Perù 1877
1593	9o	d. o.
1594	91	Rio de Janeiro. Praca de Com Pedro II. e Ilha das Cabias, Bras. 1875
1598	92	Rio de Janeiro, Bras. 1875 (Straßenansicht)
1599	93	Rio de Janeiro, Bras. 1875
16oo	94	R.D.J.: Botafogo Corcovado, Bras. 1875
16o1	95	R.d.J.: Quinta in Botafogo, Bras. 1875
16o2	96	Rio Sao Francisco:Chachoeira de Paolo Affonso, Bras. 1875
16o3	97	Bahia, Bras. 1875
16o4	98	Bahia, Untere Stadt, Bras. 1875
16o5	99	Pernambuco, Recife (mit Fotograf) Bras. 1875
16o6	1oo	Pernambuco, Einfahrt in den Hafen, Bras. 1875
16o7	1o1	d. o.
16o8	1o2	Alphons Stübel ca 19oo
16o9	1o3	d. o.

René Burri, One world. Fotografien u. Collagen 1950-1983, Bern 1984

1610 Sao Paulo, Bras. 1960
1611 Buenos Aires, Arg. 1958
1612 Buenos Aires Arg. 1960
1613 Dt. Kriegerdenkmal für die Toten der Schlacht von El Alamein Tobruk, Libyen 1955
1614 Strassenszene, Imperia Oneglia, It. 1955
1615 Patio im Haus des Arch. Luis Barragan, Mexico City 1969
1616 Bestigungsanlage auf der Klaveninsel Gorée, Senegal 1966
1617 Schaufenster bei Tokyo, Japan 1971
1618 Bordell bei Tae Song Dong, Südkorea, 1961
1619 Leonforte, Sizilien 1956
1620 Avenida Rio Branco, Rio de Janeiro, Bras. 1958
1621 Bol. Hochland 1958
1622 Lotusblüten im See beim Sommerpalast bei Peking 1964
1623 Fifth Avenue, New York 1967
1624 Gesundheitsministerium Rio de Janeiro, Bras. 1960
1625 Big Tex, Houston USA 1977
1626 Teehaus bei Teheran, Iran 1960
1627 "Die Deutschen" Brandmauern in Westberlin, 1959
1628 Betriebsfeier in Essen, BRD 1960
1629 Russ. Kriegerdenkmal in Treptow, Ostberlin 1959
1630 Reeperbahn, Hamburg 1960
1631 Ruhrgebiet 1960
1632 Wannsee, Westberlin 1961
1633 Manöver in der Lüneburger Heide, BRD 1959
1634 Ruhrgebiet 1961
1635 Beirut, Libanon 1962
1636 Regierungspalast Casa Rosada, Buenos Aires, Arg. 1958
1637 König Paul und Königin Frederike begleiten den Sarg von Prinz Georg, Athen 1957
1638 Sechstagekrieg, Mitla Paß. Sinai. 1967
1639 Suez-Kanal, Ägypten 1974
1640 Sadat und Nixon bei den Prymiden v Gizeh, Äg. 1974
1641 Rede von Fidel Castro in Havanna, Kuba 1963
1642 Unterhaltungsviertel Havanna, Kuba 1963
1643 Bordell in Than Son Nut, Saigon, Südvietnam 1973
1644 Nixon gibt seinen Rücktritt bekannt, US-TV 1974
1645 Anti-Vietnam Demonstration. Washington 1972
1646 Le Corbusier in seinem Atelier in Paris 1959
1647 Über dem bolivianischen Hochland, 1958
1648 Fort Lauderdale, Florida 1966
1649 Beduine in Nizwa, Oman 1975

Lothar Rübelt, Östrreich zwischen den Kriegen,
Wien, München, Zürich 1979 Stabi

1650 Lothar Rübelt, Sängerbundfest in Wien, Juli 1928. Ankunft des Berliner Beethovenchores

1651 Lothar Rübelt,Hochzeit in der Wiener Burgkapelle

1652 Tennisplätze am Wiener Donaukanal. Golfspieler im Wiener Prater

1653 Tennisweltmeisterin Suzanne Lenglen, 1924

1654 Hutmodell der Firma P. und C.Habig, Wien

1655 Sommerfreuden im Strandbad Kritzendorf an der Donau, 1926 Die Teilnehmer vor dem Quer-durch-Wien-Schwimmen reiben sich mit Öl ein

1656 Sonnenanbeter und "Strandgirls" in Millstatt in Kärnten,1930

1657 Bettlerautomat, 1927

1658 Arbeitslosigkeit in Steyr, 1932: Ausspeisungsaktion

1659 Arbeitslosigkeit in Steyr, 1932: Arbeitslosenunterstützungsstelle

1660 SS-Männer beim NS-Gauparteitag in Wien, Spet. 1932
NS-Kundgebung vor der Karlskirche in Wien, Nov. 1932

1661 NS-Gauparteitag in Wien 1932: Dt. Ehrengäste: Ernst Roehm, Herrmann Göring, Julius Streicher, u.li: Rede des Reichspropagandaleiters der NSDAP, Joseph Goebbels, in der Wiener Engelmann-Arena, u.re: Gauparteitag in Wien 1932: Göring, Roehm, Habicht (oben) Frauenfeld, Du Moulin-Eckart

1662 Demonstration illegaler Nationalsozialisten nach den Österr. Skimeisterschaften in Mallmütz (Kärnten)
NS-Aufmarsch in Wien 1932. Wegen Uniformverbot gehen die Nationalsozialisten ohne Braunhemd oder in weißen Hemden

1663 Frühlingsfahrt für arme Kinder. Start vor dem Wiener Rathaus, 1933

1664 Werbeautobus der Firma Philips vor dem Parlament in Wien, Werbeautobus für Papier-Zigarettenhülsen, 1927

1665 ATA-Werbung in Wien, ca 1925, Nachtaufnahme

1666 Auftanken des Flugzeugs eines dt.Teilnehmers am Europa-Rundflug in Wien-Aspern

1667 Sängerbundfest in Wien. Ankunft des Berliner Beethoven-Chores Juli 1928

1668 Filmaufnahmen der Selenophon Tonfilmschau Austria beim Semmeringrennen

1669 Tauernrennen 1927, Start zu einer Wertungsfahrt vor dem Wiener Rathaus

1670 Motorradwertungsfahrt, ADAC Wertungsfahrt

1671 Rennläuferin ca 1933

1672 Arbeiter-Massenturnen im Wiener Stadion
Arbeit-Schauturnen auf dem Wiener Rathausplatz

1673 Probe von Turnerinnen für die Teilnahme an der Arbeiterolympiade, 1931; Reifenübungen - Probe für die Teilnahme an der Arbeiterolympiade

1674 Lothar Rübelt, Durchfahrt der Deutschen Wehrmacht durch Innsbruck 12.3.1938

1675 Lothar Rübelt, Großdeutscher Tag in Wien, 9.4.1938. Die Menge in Erwartung Adolf Hitlers

1676 Lothar Rübelt, Wahlzelle bei der Volksabstimmung am 10.4.1938

1677 Lothar Rübelt, Wien

Paul Senn. Photographien aus den Jahren 1930 - 1953, Hrg. Guido Magnaguagno, Bern o.J. DSB

1678 Paul Senn, Am Turnfest , Bern 1947

1679 Pablo Casals im Casino Bern, Anfang 30er J.e

1680 Paul Senn (1901-53) Ernest Ansermet probt Strawinskys "Feuervogel", Genf 1950

1681 Senn, Charles -Ferdinand Ramuz, 1937

1682 Am Mittelmeer bei Noli, 1938

1683 Schwarzhändler vor dem Café "Au soleil levant"Paris 1945

Rudolf Kicken (Ed.), Eine Ausstellung von hundert Photographien von Heinrich Kühn, Köln 1981 DSB

1684 Heinrich Kühn (1866 - 1944) Vier Kinder, Sonnenschein, ca 1912, Gummi- und Pigmentdruck

1685 Heinrich Kühn,Tonwertstudie III (Miss Mary) 1910,Bromöldruck

1686 Kühn, Hans Kühn, ca 1906, Gummi- und Pigmentdruck

1687 Kühn, Frau Ing. Richter, mehrf.Bromölumdruck auf Japanpapier ca 1913

1688 Kühn, In Ragusa, 1906 Mehrf. Bromöldruck auf Japanpapier

1689 Kühn (Rückenakt) ca 1920, -- " --

1690 Kühn (Frauentorso im Sonnenlicht) ca 1920 -- " --

1691 Kühn,(Karaffe und Blumen) o.D., Bromöldruck

1692 Kühn,(Sonnenbild im Atelier) o.D. Mehrf. Bromöldruck

Paul Senn. Photographien 1930 - 1953

1693 Paul Senn, Paul Senn 1949

1694 Senn, Bauer aus dem Emmental während der Getreideernte, 1934

1695 Senn, Walliser Bauern, 1936

1696 Senn, Getreideernte im Emmental, 1934 (Frau)

1697 Holzarbeiterinnen im Emmental, 1941

1698 Verdingbuben in einer Anstalt des Kantons Solothurn,ca 1935

1699 Der Schlaf im Wirtshaus, 1935

1700 Schichtwechsel im Gaswerk, 1935

1701 Der Guß. Sulzer. Winterhur , ca 1940

1702 Paul Senn, Metallarbeiter, ca 1940
1703 Senn, Bauarbeiter, 1934
1704 Senn, Im Altersheim eines Jurastädtchens, ca 1935
1705 Senn, Geisteskranker im Garten der Irrenanstalt Waldau, 1936
1706 Senn, Bauernpaar aus Andalusien (Spanienkrieg)
1707 Senn, Der Schluss. Am Tag vor der Abreise aus Barcelona. Ein Verletzter der Volksfront-Armee aus Cordoba, 1937
1708 Senn, Le Perthus. Flüchtlinge warten im Mistral auf den Abtransport
1709 Senn, Span. Bauernmädchen auf der Flucht
1710 Senn, Köln 1945
1711 Senn, In der Kaiser-Wilhelm-Str. in Gelsenkirchen, 1945
1712 Senn, Im Flüchtlingslager, Deutschland 1945
1713 Senn, Vor Onkel Toms Hütte, USA 1946
1714 Senn, Zwei Matrosen auf Coney Island, 1946

Berlinische Galerie, Fotografische Sammlung:
Erich Salomon-Fotograffen 1928 - 1938, Berlin (W) 1986

1715 Salomon, Strafverteidiger Dr. Erich Frey vernimmt einen Zeugen während des Prozesses gegen den Ringverein "Immertreu", eine Berliner Verbrecherbande, Berlin 1928
1716 Salomon, Das Kabinett Heinrich Brüning (hintere Reihe, 2.v.re) im Garten der Reichskanzlei, Berlin, August 1930
1717 Die 73 jährige Reichstagsabgeordnete Clara Zetkin mit einer Besucherin im Berliner Reichstag, 1930
1718 Zwei Politikerinnen aus dem Jahr 1930: Katharina von Kardorff-Oheimb, Gattin des Reichstags-Vizepräsidenten und Ada Schmidt-Seil
1719 Im medizinischen Kolleg von Geheimrat Wilhelm His an der Berliner Universität ca 1930
1720 Marlene Dietrich telefoniert von Hollywood aus mit ihrer Tochter in Berlin, 1930
1721 Peter Salomon-Hunter, Erich Salomon überprüft die Einstellung seiner Leica-Kameras mit einem Pencillight, London 1937

Erich Salomon. Leica Fotografie 1930 - 1939, Bln W 1986
1722 USA 1930
1723 USA 1930
1724 USA 1930
1725 In der Nähe von Los Angeles, Kalif. 1930
1726 Überfahrt nach Ellis Island New York, 1930
1727 Zuschauer beim Footballspiel, Boston 1932
1728 Zuschauer beim Footballspiel, Boston 1932
1729 Im Hallenviertel, Paris 1935
1730 Im Hallenviertel, Paris 1935
1731 Im Hallenviertel, Paris 1935

Dias Fotogeschichte

1732 Erich Salomon, Im Hallenviertel, Paris 1935

1733 Salomon, Der engl. Fotograf Cecil Beaton in den Vogue Studios, Paris 1936

1734 Salomon, Schottland, ca 1935

1735 Salomon, England, ca 1935

1736 Salomon, Niederländische Abgeordnete beim Betrachten von Erich Salomons Buch "Berühmte Zeitgenossen in unbewachten Augenblicken", Den Haag, ca 1935

1737 Salomon, Richter beim Hooge Raad (Oberstes Gericht) der Niederlande, Den Haag 1936

Rencontres Internationales de la Photographie, Arles 1982
Willy Zielke. Photographies 1923 - 1937

1738 Willy Zielke (19o2 -) Pyramide (Glas) 1929

1739 Zielke, Glasplattenstapel I, 1929

174o Zielke , Glas - Licht - Raum, 1929

1741 Zielke, Glasplattenstapel, 1929

1742 Glasabstraktion VI, 1929

1743 Glasabstraktion VIII, 1929

1744 Glasverzerrung II, 1929

1745 Groß und klein (Kugeln) 1929

1746 Agfa-Variation II, ca 193o (Firmensignet)

1747 o.T., 1932 (Kerze)

1748 Kaviar-Reklame, 1934

1749 Milch, ca 1931

175o Photogramm IV, 1923

1751 o.T., Collage, ca 1931 (weibl.Akt)

1752 Akt, ca 1933

1753 Nackte mit Kaktus, ca 1932

1754 o.T., 1935 ("3 Grazien")

1755 Studie einer Tänzerin, ca 1927

1756 o.T., 1937 (Auge und Schleier)

1757 o.T., 1937 (Auge und Schleier)

1758 Porträtstudien, 1932

1759 Porträtstudien, 1932

176o o.T. 1935 (Bauarbeiten)

Repros Collection Stübel, 25.9.86

SAm 105, 28, 46
105, 19, 1; 3; 4;
~~99, 19, 20~~ (?)
99, 19, 25
99, 19, 37; 41
86, 20.1, 28
86, 20.5, 61; 63; 65 1
86, 20.7, 88; ~~90~~;
~~86, 20.8, 98~~ v
86, 20.12, 114; 118 v
21, 23.22, 38, 39, 41, 43, 45, 46
21, 23.19, 15; 21; 23
21, 21.18, 83
1, 24.10, 46; 47
1, 24.5, 18; 19 v 2
1, 24.4, 17 v
88, 8.11, 13, 14 v 3
88, 8.25, 39 v
86, 20.19, 135 v
~~79, 21.24, 1~~
59, 22.20, 80 4
59, 22.22, 91
→ 21, 23.14, 12
21, 23.13, 8; 10
21, 22.1, 1
1, 24.10a, 48 v
1, 24.7, 30
92, 20.32, 307
92, 20.33, 88; 84; 86
92, 20.26, 61
92, 20.38, 108 5

92, 20.39, 110
88, 8.8,
87, 8.2, 111
88, 9.43, 81
88, 9.70, 88
86, 20.18. 133 55
86, 20.24. 169
78, 17.36, 19
82, 12, 14, 9
77, 11.27, 98
77, 11.14, 42
73, 12.66, 3 v
51, 13.21
51, 16.35
44b, 14.47.8
34, 15, 1 (61)
21, 23.25, 59
21, 21.12. 75 v
21. 21.9, 72
21. 21.8. 71 6
21. 21.5. 68
11. 2.45, 109
110, I. 16, 63
95, 6.33, 46
92, 20.11, 58
90, 10.10, v
88, ON 1 (Concord)
88, 7.65, 18 →
88, 9.44. 77
88, 10.9.

88, 10.13
88, 9.53, 57
88, 9.72. v
77, 11.3. 16 v
74, 17.15, 41 v
62, 12.80, 15 v
51, 13.6, 25
51, 13.10, 38
51, 13.12, 36
51, 13.42
51, 13.16
39, 14.50.
44b, 14.45, 15
44b, 14.43, 18
40, 14.40, 2
40, 14.37, 4

Hank O'Neal, Berenice Abbott. Sixty Years of Photography
London 1982

1761 Berenice Abbott, Janet Flanner, 2oer Jahre
1762 René Crevel, 2oer J.
1763 James Joyce, 1926
1764 Nora Joyce, 2oer J.
1765 Djuna Barnes, 2oer J.
1766 Djuna Barnes, 2oer J.
1767 Margaret Anderson, 193o
1768 Marie Laurencin, 2oer J.
1769 Eugène Atget, 2oer J.
177o Serge Soudekian, 2oer J.
1771 Helen Tamaris
1772 Changing New York, 1929 - 1939, Washington in Union Square,
1773 Eisenbahn,
1774 Lincoln, Union Square
1775 Building New York
1776 Grundpfeiler des Rockefeller Center
1777 Gestorbener, Museum of Modern Arts, frühe 3oer J.
1778 John Watts Statue, Wall Street
1779 New York, Bowery
178o Murray Hill Hotel
1781 Trinity Church and Wall Street
1782 Brooklyn Bridge, East River
1783 New York, Bowery
1784 New York
1785 Father Duffy, Times Square
1786 Stone and William Streets
1787 Röstkorn-Mann , Orchard und Hester Streets,

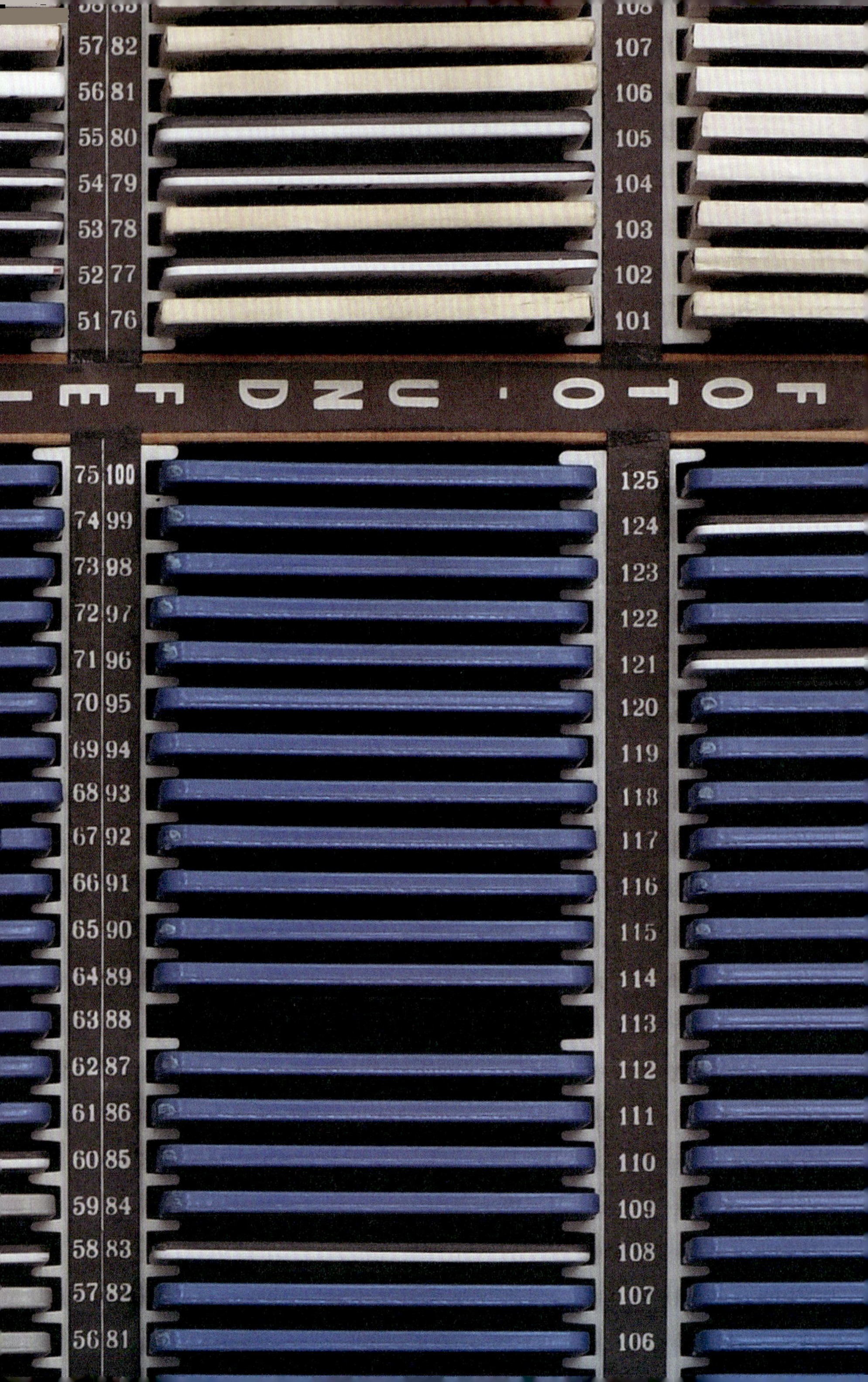
FOTO · UND FE

Kat. Quatorziemes Rencontres Intemationales de la Photographie
Albert Rudomine, Arles 1983

1788 Albert Rudomine (1892-1975) Hand v.Rodin mit Figur, 1937
1789 Rudomine, Francis Pélinier, Radweltmeister (Akt) 1926
179o Rudomine, Der Tänzer Benglia, 1921
1791 F. Gemier in der Rolle von Aristide Bruant, 1923
1792 Léon Bakst, 1937
1793 Harry Baur in "Le Dieu d'Argile"
1794 Falconetti, die Jean d'Arc von Carl Dreyer, 1929
1795 Handstudie, 1928
1796 Madame Rudomine (Akt)
1797 Aktstudie, 1932
1798 Aktstudie
1799 Studie vom Kxöxper eines Kindes, Akt, 1948
18oo Rückenakt, 1925

18o1 Willy Zielke, o.T., 1932 (Schwungrad)
18o2 Willy Zielke, o.T., 1932 (Treibrad)

Kat. Renconatres Internationales de la Photographie,
Bauhaus Photographie, Arles 1983

18o3 Florence Henri, Bauhaus Dessau, 1927
18o4 Kurt Kranz, Münderreihe, 193o/31
18o5 Kurt Kranz, Augenreihe, 193o/31
18o6 Edmund Collein oder Heinz Loew, Klavier 1927
18o7 Umbo, Berlin (Nachtaufnahme) 1931
18o8 Herbert Schürmann, Kellergang, 1931
18o9 Walter Funkat, Kugeln, 1929
181o Georg Muche, Stilleben aus Glas, 1921/22
1811 Gyula Pap, Schale, 1928
1812 An., o.T., ca 1929 (Glasstilleben)
1813 Kurt Kranz, Selbstporträt, 1932 (mit Kamera)
1814 T. Lux Feininger, Bauhausorchester, 1929
1815 Eugen Batz, o.T., 1932 (Stilleben)
1816 Grete Stern (Studio Ringl + Pit) Komal (Werbung)
1817 Florence Henri, Porträt, Paris 193o
1818 Florence Henri, Komposition, 193o
1819 Florence Henri, Stilleben, 1932 (Glas, Tisch, Frucht)

Bauhaus Photographie, Kat. Arles

1820 Imre Feher, Manege, 1935
1821 Pierre Boucher, Schraube eines Paketbootes, Normandie, o.D.
1822 René Zuber, Treppe, Normandie, o.D.
1823 René Zuber, Villa in Syrien, 1936
1824 Imre Feher, Badende, ca 1935
1825 Imre Feher, o.T., 1936, Pierre Boucher, Sportler, 1935
1826 Pierre Boucher, Isolatoren, ca 1933
1827 René Zuber, Tassen, 1934

~~1828~~
Berenice Abbott (Changing New York, 1929 - 1939)

1828 Queensboro Brücke vom Pier 41. Str. aus, Queens
1829 Broadway und Rector-Street von oben
1830 115 Jay Street, Brooklyn
1831 ~~East Side Portrait, 1947/48~~ American People and Places
1832 Lewis Hine, 40/50er Jahre
1833 Designer's Window, Bleecker Street, 50er Jahre
1834 Alter Mann auf Schaukelstuhl, 50er J.

Herlinde Koelbl, Feine Leute, 1985

1835 - 1847
Man Ray, Photographien

Reproduktionen nach den Fotografien in der Ausstellung "Man Ray. Fotografien", Leipzig 1986, Berlin 1987

1848 Man Ray, (Staubspuren)
1849 Man Ray, Karussell
1850 Man Ray, Akt
1851 Ray, (Spiegel)
1852 Ray, Akt
1853 Ray, Schwarz und Weiß, 1926 (Kiki)
1854 Ray, (verschleierter Kopf)
1855 Ray, Max Ernst, ca 1935
1856 Ray, Porträt
1857 Ray, Pablo Picasso, 1932
1858 Ray, Juan Miro
1859 Ray, (Modepuppe)

Dias Fotogeschichte

1860 Man Ray, Alexander Calder
1861 Man Ray, Alberto Giacometti
1862 Man Ray, Tristan Tzara, René Crevel
1863 Ray, André Breton
1864 (Frau in Motorradoverall)
1865 (Porträt)
1866 Giorgio de Chirico
1867 Barbette, 1926
1868 Luis Bunuel, 1929
1869 Retour à la raison, 1923
1870 Coco Chanel, ca 1935
1871 Juliet, 40er Jahre
1872 Modefotografie , 1925
1873 Modefotografie
1874 Modefotografie, 1925
1875 Integration of shadows, 1929
1876 Kiki de Montparnasse, 1922
1877 o.T. (Akt mit angewinkeltem Arm) Solarisation
1878 o.T.,(männl. Akt) Solarisation
1879 (Akt) Solarisation
1880 (New York)
1881 (Paris)
1882

Dias Fotogeschichte

Wilhelm von Gloeden (1856-1931), Fotografien aus der Sammlung der HGB/Bibliothek

1883 Wilhelm von Gloeden, Zwei Knaben
1884 Gloeden, männl. Akademie
1885 Knabe
1886 männl. Akademie
1887 Antike Szenerie (5 Knaben)
1888 Zwei Knaben
1889 Knabe
1890 Knabe als antike Gottheit
1891 Drei Knaben
1892 Zwei Knaben (Paar)
1893 Knabe vor bemaltem Vorhang
1894 Zwei Knaben
1895 Knabe
1896 Knabe
1897 "Antike Szene"
Zielke, Willy
1898 Willy Zielke, Stilleben, ca 1933 color
1899 Willy Zielke, ca 1933, Stilleben, color
1900 Zielke, Akt, 1933 color
1901 Zielke, Akt, 1933 color

Modephotographien aus "Phototechnik" 1986

1902 Horst P. Horst, Modefoto Vogue, 1940 color
1903 John Rawlings, Modefoto Vogue, ca 1945
1904 Toni Frissell, Modefoto Vogue, 1939
1905 Toni Frissell, Modefoto Vogue, vor 1942
1906 John Rawlings, Modefoto Vogue, Ende der 30er Jahre
1907 Louise Pahl-Wolfe, Modefoto Vogue, 30er Jahre

Doon Arbus, Marvin Israel (Hrg), diane arbus, New York, 1972
ZB/VBK

1908 Stephen Frank, Diane Arbus 1970
1909 Diane Arbus (1923-1971) Russ. Liliputaner in einem Wohnzimmer, New York, 1963
1910
1911 Arbus, Junger Mann mit Lockenwicklern, New York, 1966
1912 Arbus, Mädchen mit Zigarre im Washington Square Garden, New York, 1965
1913 Arbus, Mexikanischer Liliputaner in seinem Hotelzimmer, New York, 1970

Dias Fotogeschichte

1913 Diane Arbus, Eine junge Familie aus Brooklyn beim Sonntags-
ausflug, New Yor, 1966
1914 Arbus, Puertorikanische Frau mit Schönheitsfleck, New Y. 1965
1915 Arbus, Junge mit Strohut vor dem Beginn einer Parade für
den Krieg, New York 1967
1916 Arbus, Blumenmädchen bei einer Hochzeit, Connecticut 1964
1917 Arbus, Ein jüdischer Riese zu Hause in der Bronx, New York 197o
1918 Eineiige Zwillinge, New Jersey 1967
1919 Zwei tanzende Männer auf einem Transvestiten-Ball, New York 197o
192o Ein Ehepaar im Wald bei einem Nudisten-Camp, New Jersey 1963
1921 Weinendes Kind, New Jersey 1967
1922 Ein junger Mann und seine Freundin mit Hot Dogs im Park,
New York 1971
1923 Transvestit während der Geburtstagsparty, New York 1969
1924 Frau mit Medaille im Washington Squre Park, New York 1965
1925 Burlesk-Schauspielerin in ihrer Garderobe, Atlantic City,
New York, 1963
1926 Drillinge in ihrem Schlafzimmer, New Jersey, 1963
1927 Eine Frau mit Perlenkette und Ohrgehänge, New Yor, 1967
1928 Mann bei einer Parade in der Fifth Avenue, New Yor, 1969
1929 Ein junger Mann und seine schwangere Frau im Washington
New York, 1965
193o Hermaphrodit und Hund im Wohnwagen auf einem Rummelplatz
Maryland, 197o
1931 Nudistin mit Schwan-Sonnenbrille, Pannsylvania 1965
1932 Topless-Tänzerin in ihrer Garderobe, SanFrancisco, 1968
1933 Patriotischer junger Mann mit Fahne, New York 1967
1934 Junges Pärchen in der Hudson Street, New York 1963
1935 Mädchen mit entblößtem Oberkörper auf i.Bett, N.Y. 1968
1936 Ballkönig u.-königin einer Tanzveranstaltung für ältere
Bürger, New Yor, 197o
1937 Teilnehmer an einem Bodybuilding-Wettbewerb, New York 1968
1938 Kind mit Spielzeug-Handgranate im Central Park, New York 1962
1939 Zwei Mädchen mit gleichen Badeanzügen, Coney Island,N.Y. 1967
194o Ein Mädchen in seinem Zirkuskostüm, Maryland 197o
1941 Mutter mit Kind, New Jersey 1967
1942 Sitzender Mann mit BHund Nylons, New York 1967
1943 Mann mit Indianer-Kopfschmuck, New York 1969
1944 Frau mit Schleier in der Fifth-Avenue, New Yor, 1969
1945 Nackter Mann als Frau posierend, New Yor, 1968
1946 Transvestit auf einem Kostümball, New York 197o

Dias Fotogeschichte

D

1947 Diane Arbus, Transvestit auf einem Kostümball, NY 1970

1948 Diane Arbus, Eine Frau mit Affenbaby, New Jersey 1971

1949 Arbus,Frau mit Pelzkragen auf der Straße, New York 1968

1950 Frau in Negligé, New York 1966

1951 Tätowierter Mann auf einem Rummelplatz, Maryland 1970

1952 Mädchen in einem Satinkleid, New York 1967

1953 Zwei Freunde zu Hause, New York 1965

1954 Transvestit mit eingerissenem Strumpf, New York 1966

1955 o.T. (Serie mit Aufnahmen von geistig Behinderten) 1970/71

1956 o.T.

1957 o.T.

1958 o.T.

1959 Petal Pink for little parties, White-over-pale for parties,1962

1960 Norman Mailer, 1963

1961 William Golding, 1963

1962 Mildred Dunnock, 1964

1963 Mrs. T. Charlton Henry, Chestnut Hill, Philadelphia, 1965

Karl Blossfeld, Urformen der Kunst, Berlin 1928

1964 Blossfeld, Erynbium giganteum. Männertreu. Blütenköpfchen mit Hüllblättern in 4 f Vergrößerung

1965 Blossfeld,Asclepias speciosa. Seidenpflanze, Blüte in 10f Vergr.

1966 Symphytum officinale. Schwarzwurz, Blüte in 25 Vergr.

1967 Scabiosa columbaria. Tauben-Skabiose.Samenköpfchen in 10f Vergr.

1968 Acanthus mollis. Akanthus, Bärenklau. Deckblätter, die Blüten sind entfernt, in 4 f Vergr.

1969 Abutilon. Linden-Malve. Samenkapseln in 6 f Vergr.

1970 Asclepias speciosa. Seidenpflanze.Blütendolde in 3 f Vergr.

1971 Achillea clypeolata. Schafgarbe. Trugdolde in 15 f Vergr.

1972 Aspidium filix mas. Wurmfarn. Junge gerollte Blätter in 4 f V.

1973 Serratula nudicaulis. Nacktstengelige Scharte.Samenköpfchen in 5 f Vergr.

1974 Aconitum. Eisenhut. Junger Sproß in 6 f Vergr.

1975 Equisetum hiemale. Winter-Schachtelhalm. Jg. Sproß in 25 F. V.

1976 Geum rivale. Bach-Nelkenwurz. Blütenknospe, die Kelchblätter sind entfernt, in 25 f Vergr.

1977 Equisetum hiemale. Winter-Schachtelhalm. Querschnitt eines Stengels in 30f Vergr.

1978 -- " -- . Winter - Schachtelhalm

1979 Karl Blossfeldt, Equisetum hiemale. Winterschachtelhalm. Wurzelstück in 8 f Vergr.

1980 Blossfeldt, Silphium laciniatum. Kompaßpflanze. Ein am Stengel getrocknetes Blatt in 5 f Vergr.

1981 Delphium. Rittersporn. Teil eines getrockneten Blattes in 6 f Vergr.

Alfred Eisenstaedt: Eisenstaedt. Deutschland, New York 1981 HGB

1982 Eisenstaedt, Marlene Dietrich, Ende der 2oer Jahre

1983 Eisenstaedt, Radfahrer am Holsteiner Ufer, Berlin 1928

1984 Luis Trenker, Davos, Schweiz 1932

1985 Graf Zeppelin wird auf dem Flug nach Rio de Janeiro über dem Südatlantic repariert, 1934

1986 Graf Zeppelin liegt verankert, Recife, Pernambuco, Bras. 1934

1987 Orsenigo, der päpstliche Nuntius in Dt. in Hotel Adlon, Berlin 1932, rechts Reichskanzler Heinrich Brüning,

1988 Propagandaminister Joseph Goebbels mit seinem Privatsekretär und Hitlers Dolmetscher bei der 15. Generalversammlung des Völkerbunds in Genf, Sept. 1933

1989 Hindenburgs Begräbnis, Tannenberg, August 1934

1990 Marlene Dietrich, Anna May Wong, Leni Riefenstahl auf dem Ball der Kunstschule Reimann im Marmorsaal, Berlin 1928

1991 Turnlehrer auf der Insel Hiddensee bei Rügen, 1931

1992 Generaloberst Werner von Blomberg, Chef des Generalstabs unter einem Bildnis von Hermann Göring im Generalstab, Berlin 1934

1993 Truempy-Ballet-Schule, Berlin 1931

1994 Herbert Bayer, Profile en face, 1929

1995 Paul Wolff, New York, 1932 (Nachtaufnahme)

1996 Hans Finsler, Eier im Raum, 195o

1997 Jean Pierre Sudre, Le Civet, Merville (Hasenklein) 1953

1998 Adolf Lazi, Studie mit Würfel, ca 195o

1999 Rolf Winquist, Frauenporträt, vor 1957

2000 Reinhart Wolf, Die Schauspielerin Xenia Hagemann, München 1955

2001 Paul Wolff, Manhattan, Court Yard, 1945

2002 Alfred Eisenstaedt, Leni Riefenstahl, München, März 198o

Dias Fotogeschichte

Valentine Lawford, Horst. His Work and his World, VIKING,Penguin Books Ltd., Harmondsworth, Middlesex, 1984, IfÄK

2oo3 George Hoyningen-Huene, Horst P. Horst, Paris 1931

2oo4 Horst P. Horst, Hoyningen-Huene, Paris 193o

2oo5 Cecil Beaton, Hoyningen-Huene, ca 1929

2oo6 Hoyningen-Huene, Horst P. Horst

2oo7 Hoyningen-Huene, Cecil Beaton, Ashcombe, 193o

2oo8 Horst, Allan Pryce-Jones, 1932 (novelist and socialhistorian)

2oo9 Horst, William Etting, Paris 1932

2o10 Horst, Hutmode, Paris 1933

Carl Haenlein, (Hrg) Hans Bellmer. Photographien, Kestner-Ges. Hannover 1984, DSB

2o11 Hans Bellmer (19o2 - 1975) Die Puppe, 1935 - 37

2o12 Hans Bellmer, H.B. und die Puppe aus der Edition von 1934

2o13 - 2o39 Hans Bellmer, Die Puppe, 1935 - 37

2o4o Hans Bellmer, o.T., 1946 (Pornographie)

2o41 Hans Bellmer, o.T., 1946 (Pornographie)

2o42- 2o48 Hans Bellmer, Unica (Unica Zürn) , 1958, (Einschnürungen)

Dias Fotogeschichte

Horst P. Horst. His work and his world, ed. by Valentine Lawford
Viking. Penguin Books Ltd. Hammondsworth, Middlesex 1985

2003 Hoyningen-Huene, Horst P. Horst, Paris 1931
2004 George Hoyningen-Huene, Paris 1930
2005 Cecil Beaton, Hoyningen-Huene, 1929
2006 Hoyningen-Huene, Horst P. Horst als griech. Plastik, 1930
2007 -- " --
2008 Hoyningen-Huene, Cecil Beaton, Ashcombe, 1930
2009 Horst P. Horst, Allan Pryce-Jones, 1932
2010 Horst P. Horst, William Etting, Paris 1932
2011 Modephotographie, Paris 1933
2012 [49] Lee Miller, Paris 1932
2013 [50] Bette Davis, New York 1932
2014 [51] Toni Frissell
2015 [52] Mistinguett, Paris 1934
1016 [53] Brigitte Helm als Antinea
2017 [54] Gerald Kelly, Foto von Hoyningen-Huene
2018 [55] Horst P. Horst, Baron Nicolas de Gunzburg, Paris 1934
2019 [56] Horst, Vicomtesse de Noailles, Paris 1934
2020 [57] Elsa Schiaparelli, Paris 1936
2021 [58] French Vogue, 1935
2022 [59] French Vogue, 1935 Paris
2023 [60] Vogue, New York 1935
2024 [61] Vogue, New York 1935
2025 [62] French Vogue, Paris 1936
2026 [63] Clare Boothe Luce, New York, 1936
2027 [64] Modellphoto für French u. Am. Vogue, Paris 1935
2028 [65] Luchino Visconti, Hammamet, Tunesien, 1935
2029 [66] Vogue, Paris 1936
2030 [67] Photo für Mainbocher, Paris 1936
2031 [68] French Vogue, Paris 1937
2032 [69] Chanel, Paris 1937
2033 [70] Stilleben, New York 1937
2034 [71] Stilleben i.d. Vogue Studios, Paris 1937
2035 [72] Akt (Lisa Fonssagrives), Paris 1938
2036 [73] Horst, Hutmodell (Lisa Fonssagrives) Paris 1938
2037 [74] Horst, Joan Crawford, New York 1938
75

Horst P. Horst

2o74 French Vogue, 1937, Zelinsky
2o75 Vogue, New York, 1938
2o76 Mainbocher Korsett, 1939, Paris
2o77 Luchino Visconti, Paris 1935
2o78 Kostüme, entworfen von Dali für das Ballett Bacchanale,
ausgeführt von Chanel, Paris 1939
2o79 Horst, Vogue Cover, April 1939, Helen Benett
2o80 Vogue, 1939
2o81 Myrna Loy, New York 1942
2o82 Dolores del Rio (Schauspielerin), New York 1942
2o83 Duches of Windsor in den Vogue studios, NewYork, 194o
2o84 Vogue 1942
2o85 Vogue, Merle Oberon, New York 1942
2o86 French and Am. Vogue, 1938
2o87 French Vogue, 1938
2o88 Vogue, New York 1938
2o89 Stilleben, Paris 1939
2o9o Stilleben
2o91 Ginger Rogers, 1935
2o92 Porträt
2o93 Marlene Dietrich im Vogue Studio, New York, 1942
2o94 Gertrude Stein und ihr Hund Basket, Paris 1946
2o95 Marlene Dietrich und ihre Tochter, Vogue studio, 1947
2o96 Edith Sitwell, Vogue studio, New York 1948
2o97 Vogue 1948
2o98 Vogue 1951
2o99 Vogue 195o
2100 Luchino Visconti, Rom 1953
21o1 Schwarzer Akt, New York 1953

Dias Fotogeschichte

Rainer Fabian/Hans Christian Adam, Masters of Early Travel Photography, Thames and Hudson, London 1983

2102 Francis Frith (1822-1898) Säulenhalle in Karnak, 1857
2103 Frith, Gestürzte Statue Ramses II. in Theben, 1857
2104 Frith, Kolosse in der Nubischen Wüste, 1857
2105 Frith, Kalifengräber vor Kairo, ca 1857
2106 Frith, Tempel auf der Insel Philae, Boot des Fotografen,1857
2107 Maxime DuCamp, Statue Ramses des Großen in Abu Simbel, 1850
2108 Frith, Bas-Relief im Gr. Tempel von Philae, 1857
2109 Frith, Löwenkopf am Äußeren des Tempels v. Dendera, 1857
2110 Dunmore &Critcherson, Eisberge im Baffin's Bay, 1869
2111 Dunmore & Critcherson, --"--
2112 Baron Stillfried (?) Doppelporträt (Japan) ca 1880
2113 Felice Beato, Japan. Offizier, ca 1875
2114 Anon., Harakiri im Studio, ca 1890
2115 Kusakabe Kimbei, Buddist. Mönch, ca 1885
2116 Anon, Jap. Gruß-Zeremonie, ca 1885
2117 Kusakabe Kimbei, Geisha, ca 1880
2118 Baron Stillfried, Regenschauer im Atelier, ca 1875
2119 Kimbei, Feuerwehrleute auf dem Neujahrsfestival, ca 1890
2120 Anon, Menschl. Pyramide, ca 1890
2121 Baron Stillfried, Akrobatenkind mit Feder-Kopfschmuck, ca 1880
2122 Anon., Gymnastik, ca 1885
2123 Anon, Tätowierter, ca 1880
2124 Stillfried, Samurais vor gemaltem Hintergrund, ca 1880
2125 Marc Ferrez, Botokuden-Indianer in der Provinz Bahia, 1875
2126 Samuel Bourne, Tor zum Luchnow - Bazaar, 1865
2127 Bourne &Shepherd, Maharadscha von Rewah, ca 1877
2128 Bourne, Inneres der Moschee von Agra, 1865
2129 Bourne, Skulpturen der Tempelfassade in Trichinopoly,ca 1869
2130 Bourne, Pass im Himalaya, 1866
2131 John Thomson, Todelkäfig, ca 1870
2132 John Thomson (1837-1921) "Lilienfuß" ca 1870
2133 Thomson, Einer von der Stadtwache, 1871

Dias Fotogeschichte

2134 John Thomson,Chines. Mädchen, ca 1868
2135 John Thomson, Vornehme Chinesin, ca 1868
2136 Thomson, General-Statthalter der 2 Kwang-Provinzen, ca 1871
2137 Thomson, Bettler-König und seine Bediensteten im Hafenviertel von Fuchow, ca 1870
2138 Thomson, Chines. Bergleute, ca 1870
2139 Thomson, Chines. Kuli, ca 1870
2140 Thomson, Greisin, ca 1870
2141 Thomson, Künstler aus Hong-Kong in seinem Atelier, ca 1868
2142

Album "Orient", ca 1900 aus dem Besitz von Michael Scheffer,Leipzig

2142 Musiker, Wahrsagerin (Halbakt)
2143 Türk.(?) Frau
2144 Drogman, Reiseführer, Bonfils
2145 L. Fiorillo, Türk. Sergant
2146 Bonfils, Arab. Musiker in Jerusalem
2147 Frau auf einer Schaukel
2148 Arnoux, Erste Tänzerin des Theaters Kédivial, Kairo
2149 2150 Arnoux, Tänzerin
2151 Frau in oriental. Tracht
2152 Arnoux, Wasserträgerin des Serail
2153 Arnoux, Geliebte des Sultans
2154 Türk. Frau nach Verlassen des Bades
2155 Halbakt
2156 Frau auf Diwan mit Wasserpfeife, Arnoux
2157 Arnoux, Kostümierte Bayadère
Arnoux, Dienerin eines arab. Cafés

Dias Fotogeschichte

2158 Herbert Bayer, Photoplastik, 1936 (?)
2159 Grete Back, Doppelporträt, 1930
2160 Florence Henri, Komposition mit Tellern, 1931
2161 Florence Henri, Komposition mit Schalen, 30er J.
2162 Friedrich Victor Spitzer, Gustav Klimt, 1905
Hugo Erfurth, Mädchen mit Hut, vor 1902
2163 Horst P. Horst, Verushka, Vogue, 1962
2164 Horst P. Horst, Schiaparelli dress, Vogue, 1940
2165 Horst P. Horst, Castillo dress, Vogue , 1939
2166 Horst P. Horst, Lissa Fonssagrives, Vogue, 1940er
2167

Paul Wolff, "Arbeit"
2168 - 2185

Bruce Bernard, Photodiscorery, London
2186 Charles Simart, Weibl. Akt, ca 1850, Salzpapier
2187 d.o., Männl. Akt, ca 1850, Salzpapier
2188 Rev. Calvert Jones, Florence, 1845-46, (?)
2189 Edouard Duseigneur, Schneider, frühe 50er, Salzpapier
2190 An, Akte, ca 1850, Dag.
2191 An., Alter Veteran und seine Frau, 1860 Ambrotypie
2192 Roger Fenton, Odalisque, 1858, Salzpapier
2193 Desiré Charnay, Chichen - Itza, ca 1860, Ap
2194 An., Akt, 1850er Dag.
2195 An., Akt, 1850er Dag.,
2196 Auguste Salzmann, Kaktus und Säule, Jerusalem, 1854
2197 Braquehais, Akt mit Schleier, 1854
2198 An., Schmied, 1850er Dag.
2199 Baldus, Privathaus, ca 1855
2200 Jean Charles Langlois, Schlachtfeld von Sebastopol, 1855
2201 An., Dienerin, 1850er Dag.
2202 Julia Margaret Cameron, Mary Hillier, ca 1862
2203 Nadar, Nadar und Madame N. und Sohn, 1865 Ap
2204 Collard, Rundhaus, Nevers, 1862-67, Ap (der Eisenbahn)
2205 Camille Silvy, Straßenmusikanten, London, ca 1860 Ap
2206 Hippolyte Bayard, Selbstbildnis als Ertrunkener, 1840
2207 Southworth/Hawes, Alte Frau, 1850er Dag.
2208 Henri Le Secq, Kathedrale von Chartres, 1852, Photolithographie
2209 Talbot, Zimmerleute auf den Gut Lacock, 1842
2210 Gustav Oehme, Drei Mädchen, Berlin 1849, Dag.
2211 John Mc Cosh, Burmesisches Mädchen, 1857

2112 Baron Gros, Propyläen, 1850, Dag.

2113 D.O.Hill/R. Adamson, Newhavener Lotse, ca 1844

2114 Robert MacPherson, Titusbogen, Rom 1865, Ap

2115 Captain Linnaeus Tripe, Tempelfestung, Südindien, Wachspap.

2116 Nadar, Porträt von Napp (?)

2117 An.(Dt.) Porträt, späte 40er , Dag.

Erika und Fritz Kempe. Heinz Spielmann,
2118 Die Kunst der Camera im Jugendstil, Umschau-Verlag, Frankfurt am Main 1986 ISBN 3-524-68012-7

2118 Arthur Benda, Hutmodell, entworfen vom Maler Krieser, 1910

2119 Gauguin - Jacob ringt mit dem Engel, 1888 und
Demachy, In der Bretagne, 1904

2120 James Craig Annan, The White House, 1910

2121 Edward Steichen, In Memoriam, 1906 (Akt)

2122 ~~2123~~ Adolph de Meyer, Mrs. Wiggens of Belgrave Square, 1912

2124 Alvin Langdon Coburn, Brücke in Venedig, 1908

2125 Gustav Trinks, Farbige Schatten, 1902

2126 H. W. Müller, Mondnacht, 1903

2127 James Craig Annan, Frau Muthesius, 1905

2128 A. Böhm, Wellenbrecher, Rügen, 1899

2129 Constant Puyo, Montmartre, 1906

2130 James Craig Annan, Durchblick, 1900

2131 Hugo Erfurth, Dame in Schwarz, o.J.

2132 Clarence H. White, Beneath the Wrinkle (jg.Mädchen mit Großeltern) 1905

2133 Albert Gottheil, Im Hafen 1899

2134 Gertrude Käsebier, Miss N., 1903

2135 Nicola Perscheid, Herta Juhl, 1899

2136 Jacob Hilsdorf, Cosima Wagner, ca 1900

2137 Rudolf Eickemeyer jun, Im Bott, 1893

2138 Henry Peach Robinson, Morgennebel, 1902

2139 Clarence H. White/Stieglitz, Torso, 1909 (Halkakt)

Gertrude Käsebier, o.T. (Mutter mit Kindern), 1903

2240 René Le Bégue, Studie, 1906 (Akt)
2241 Arthur Benda, Elsa Kasimir, 1908
2242 Anton J. Chr. Bruhn, Schlachter und Kleinmädchen, 1908
2243 Arthur Benda, Rotes Haar, 1911
2244 A. Böhmer, Oppeln im Frühnebel, 1899
2245 Hans Watzek, Das weiße Segel, 1901
2246 Theodor und Oskar Hofmeister, Einsamer Reiter, 1903
2247 Arthur Benda, Dame, 1911
2248 Th.u.O.Hofmeister, Auf der Brücke, 1898
2249 Aura Hertwig, Gerhard Hauptmann, 1900
2250 Edward Steichen, Versailles Nocturne, 1913
2251 Arthur Benda, Mela Köhler, 1912
2252 Robert Demachy, Hinter der Bühne, 1906 (Tänzerin)
2253 Heinrich Kühn, Spielende Kinder, 1908
2254 Hugo Henneberg, Der Weiher, 1899
2255 Alfred Stieglitz, The City of Ambition, 1910(N.Y.,Ehrgeiz)
2256 Edward Steichen, The Flatiron, 1906 (Hochhaus)
2257 Alice Boughton, Jahreszeiten, 1909
2258 Alfred Stieglitz, Fähre, 1910
2259 Hugo Henneberg, Der See, 1896
2260 Heinrich Kühn, Stilleben mit Tomaten, o.J.
2261 Otto Scharf, o.T., 1901 (Ldsch. mit Bach)
2262 Rudolf Dührkoop, Peter Behrens, 1908
2263 Nicola Perscheid, Frl. Jungmann, 1900 (Freilichtporträt)
2264 Alvin Langdon Coburn, London Bridge, 1905
2265 Hugo Henneberg, Katharinen Fleet, Amsterdam, 1896
2266 Alfred Stieglitz, Das Zwischendeck, 1907
2267 Leonard Misonne, Staubiger Weg, 1897
2268 Th.u.O.Hofmeister, Sommernachmittag, 1902 (Ldsch.mit Mühle)
2269 Hugo Erfurth, Walter Tiemann,1912
2270 Pierre Dubrieul, Le Bendicte, 1902 (Kind am Tisch)
2271 Nicola Perscheid, Der Schnitter, 1902
2272 Robert Demachy, In Britannien, 1904
2273 H.W. Müller, Marine, 1900
2274 Frank Meadow Sutcliff, Im Hafen, 1897
2275 Alexis Mazourine, o.T., 1899 (Flußlandsch. mit Bäumen)
2276 Adolph de Meyer, Stilleben, 1908
2277 Maurice Brimand, o.T., 1897 (Dame mit Schleiern)
2278 Edward Steichen, Houseboat, 1908

Dias Fotogeschichte

2279 Arthur Benda, Die gelbe Jacke, 1923
2280 Minja Diez-Dührkoop, Zwei Frauen im Obstgarten, 1906
2281 James Page Croft, Drei liegende Akte, 1903
2282 Aura Hertwig, Goldene Jugend, 1899
2283 Hugo Hennberg, Birken, 1896
2284 Hugo Erfurth, Heinrich Vogeler, ca 1912
2285 Edward Steichen, Grand Stand - Steeplechase Day, Paris 1904/13
2286 Rudolf Eickemeyer, o.T., 1893
2287 Rudolf Dührkoop, Gertrud und Ursula Falke, 1906
2288 L. Alexandre, o.T., o.J. (Segelboot im Abendlicht)
2289 Frederick H. Evans, Kathedrale in New York, 1903
2290 Edward Steichen, Vitalität - Yvette Guilbert, 1913
2291 Clarence H. White, Ringspiel, 1903
2292 Alvin Langdon Coburn, Notre Dame, 1908
2293 Leonard Misonne, o.T., 1902
2294 Edward Steichen, Lady H., 1913
2295 Frederick Hollyer, Walter Crane, 1902
2296 Minya Diez-Dührkoop, Gertrud Falke, 1908
2297 George H. Seeley, Geburt von Rom, 1907 (2 Frauen)
2298 Alfred Stieglitz, Paris 1911
2299 Rudolf Dührkoop, Frau Muthesius mit ihren Kindern am Klavier, 1908
2300 Julia Margaret Cameron, Sir Henry Taylor, 1867
2301 J.M. Cameron, Waldnymphe - Seet Liberty, 1870

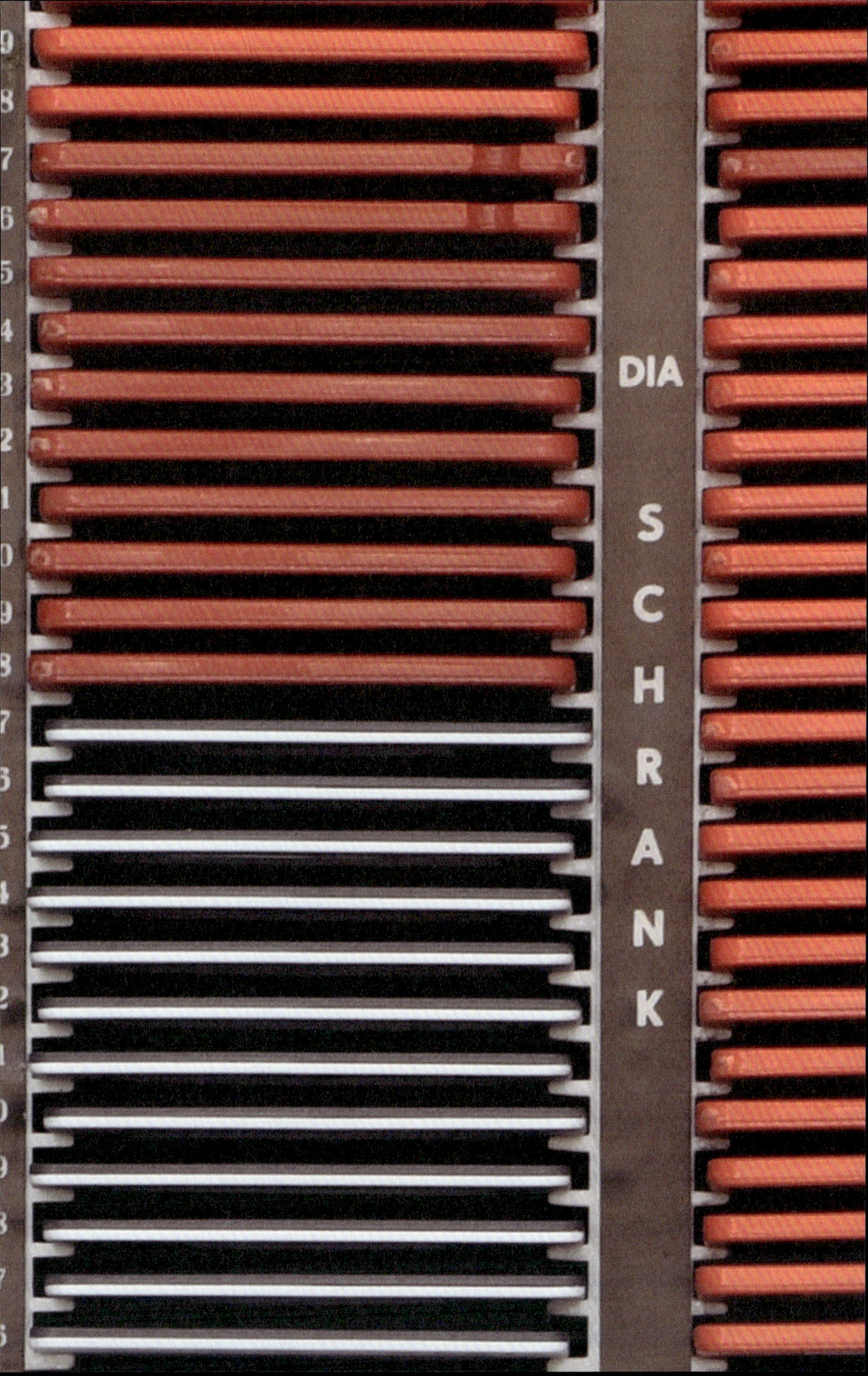
DIA
SCHRANK

Helmut Gernsheim, The Origins of Photography, London 1982

2302 Nicéphore Nièpce, Blick auf den Hof des Anwesens in Gras, 1826-27
2303 Daguerre oder Nièpce de Saint-Victor, Tafel , für ein Mahl vorbereitet, ca 1929, Phot. auf Glasgrundlage, zerst.
2304 erster Raubdruck von Daguerres Manual durch die Susse-Brüder, erschienen 6 Tage vor Giroux Edition, 6. September 1839
Aragos Bericht über den Daguerreotype, veröff. 31. Aug. 1839
Titelseite von Isidore Nièpce Broschüre, 1841
1f s.ff Louis Jacques Mandé Daguerre, Boulevard du Temple, (heute München)
2305 Daguerre (whrsch.) An. Porträt, whrsch. Charles Arrowsmith, Ass von Daguerre, ca 1842-43, Dag.
2306 William Henry Fox Talbot, Fotogramm, 1840
2307 Talbot, Fotogramm, Spitzen, Fotogramm mit Federn, 1842/1839
2308 Hippolyte Bayard, Federn, 1839, Direktpositive
2309 Bayard, Anfang der Rue Tholozé unterhalb der Windmühle "La Galette", 1843
2310 Alphons Louis Poitevin, Ansicht von Thun, 1843, Dag.
2311 An. (Dan) Porträt von Thorvaldsen, 1842-43
2312 An. (fr.), Porträt eines Jungen, ca 1845
2313 Hippolyte Fizeau, St. Louis-des-Invalides, ca 1840
2314 An. (Fr.) Wache auf dem Hof der Tuilierien, Paris, 1842-8 Dag.
2315 Léon Foucault, Weinrebe, 1844, Dag.
2316 Hill und Adamson, 8 Minister der Kirche von Schottland, Mai 1843
2317 Hill und Adamson, Rev. George Gillfillan und Dr. Samuel Brown, 43-5
2318 Hill und Adamson, Porträt einer Lady, 1843.- 5, Kal.
2319 Hill und Adamson, Seeleute in Newhaven, ca 1843-5
2320 Hill und Adamson, Steinmetze bei d Arbeit am Scott-Denkmal, 1845
2321 Hill und Adamson, Wohnhaus in Newhaven, 1845
2322 Hill und Adamson, Fischerweiber in Newhaven, ca 1845, Kal.
2323 William Henry Fox Talbot, Seine Töchter im Garten, 1842
2324 Talbot, Rankenblätter, ca 1839, Mikrophot.ie mit Sonnenmikroskop, 1839-41, Muschel, 1841-42, Kal
2325 Talbot, Hüte, ca 1844, Kal.
2326 Talbot, Kloster Lacock Abbey mit Rev. Calvert Jones, ca 1843
2327 Talbots Atelier in Reading, ca 1845, Kal. zweiteilig
2328 Talbot, Baum im Winter, 1842
2329 Talbot, Blick auf das Haus gegenüber seinem Hotel in Paris, Mai 43
2330 Talbot, Offene Tür, 1843, Kal., Pencil of Nature,
2331 Talbot, Brücke in Orleans, 1843 Kal.
2332 Talbot, Die Leiter (Pencil of Nature) 1844, Kal
2333 Hill und Adamson, Bildhauer John Stevens neben einer römischen
2334 Büste, 1843-45, Kal.

Jean - Luc Daval, Die Photographie. Geschichte einer Kunst, Aarau, Stuttgart 1983

2335 Daguerre (1787-1851) Die Seine und die Tuilerien, 1839, Dag.

2336 William Henry Fox Talbot (1800-1877) Lektüre, 1841, Kal.

2337 Nadar, (1820-1910), Selbstporträt, 1854-55, Koll, Salzpap.kop.

2338 Corot

2339 Etienne Carjat (1828-1906), Sarah Bernardt, Koll

2340 Charles Nègre(1820-1880), Paris, Marktszene am Hafen unterhalb des Rathauses, Öl. o.D

1 f s.u. Nègre, Paris, Marktszene ..., 1851, Papierneg., Salzpapierk.

2341 Gustave Le Gray (1828-1862) Ein Sonneneffekt-Ozean, 1856, Koll

2342 Grosser Säulensaal in Karnak, Theben. Aquatinta nach einer Daguerreotypie für Panorama d'Egypte et de Nubie von Hector Horeau, Paris 1841

2343 Maxime Du Camp (1822-1894) Karnak, Theben. Eingang zum grossen Säulensaal, 1852, Papierneg.

2344 An., Jane Morris sitzt Modell für D.G. Rosetti, 1865
Rosetti(1828-1882) Beatrix, um 1863, Öl

2345 Julia Margaret Cameron (1815-1879), Enid, Emily Peacock, Ill. für Alfred Tennyson, Idylls of the King, London 1874, Alb.

2346 Cameron, Lancelot und Guinevere, William Warder an May Prinsep, Ill. für Tennyson, s.o., Alb., 1874

2347 Louis Ducos du Hauron (1837 - 1920) Ansicht, Dreifarbenfot., 1878

2348 Louis Lumière (1864-1948), Das junge Mädchen und der Flieder, 1906-10, Autochromplatte

2349 Jacques Henri Lartigue(1896-1986), Gebiet von Pau, 1912, Autochromplatte

2350 Oscar Gustav Rejlander, (1813-1875) Allegorie des Lebens, 1857, Montage

2351 Lewis Carroll (1832-1898), Beatrice Henley, 1862 und

2352 John Everett Millais (1829-1896), Herbstlaub, Ausschnitt, 1865, Öl

Helmut Gernsheim, The Origins ...

2353 An., Halbakt auf einem Diwan liegend, ca 1852, kol.Stereodag.

2354 An, Chestnut Street in Philadelphia , ca 1844, Dag.

2355 John William Draper, Porträt s. Schwester, Dorothy Catherine Juni 1840, Dag.

1f 2356 An., Sammlung von Schmetterlingen, ca 1850

2357 Southworth und Hawes, Erste Op unter Betäubung, Massachusetts Generalhospital, Boston 1847, Dag.

2358 Richard Beard, Sitzender Gentleman, 1849, Dag., GB

2359 Antoine Claudet, Porträt einer Lady, ca 1850, Dag.

2360 William Telfer, ?, Alte Frau, ca 1848, Dag.

2361 William Telfer, Porträt einer Lady mit Hut, ca 1849, Dag.

2362 John Jabez Edwin Mayall, Kristall Palast, London 1851

2363 An., Porträt einer Lady, Stereodag., o.D.
2364 William Kilburn, Porträt eines Offiziers, 1853, Dag.
2365 Carl Ferd. Stelzner, Hamburger Künstler-Verein, Mai 1843
2366 Stelzner, Ruinen von Hamburg nach dem gr. Brand, Mai 1842
2367 Antoine Claudet, Lady Isabella Stevens, ca 1852, Stereodag.
2368 D.O. Hill, Porträt von Robert Adamson, ca 1843, Kal.
2369 Daguerre, Stilleben, 1837-39 , Dag.
237o Daguerre, Komposition mit Muscheln, 1837
2371 Daguerre, Notre Dame und das hist. Zentrum v. Paris, 1838/39D
2372 Daguerre, Boulevard du Temple, 1839, Dag.
2373 John Shaw Smith, Relief am Tempel in Theben, 1851
2374 John Wistler, Altes Bauernhaus, 1852
2375 Alois Löcherer, Transport der Kolossal-Statue der Bavaria in München, 185o,Wachsp.

Erna Lendvai-Dircksen, Das Deutsche Volksgesicht

2376 - Titel
2413 Lendvai-Dircksen, Bildnisse aus "Das Deutsche Volksgesicht"

Erna Lendvai-Dircksen, Bildnisse aus " Das Germanische Volksgesicht"

2414 - Flandern 1942
2423 Lendvai - Dircksen, Bildnisse (Masuren)

Carl Heinrich Stratz, Die Darstellung des menschlichen Körpers in der Kunst, Berlin 1914 (3.u.4.Tausend)

2424 Hermes des Praxiteles, Plastik
2425 Torso eines italien. Jünglings, von 16 Jahren, Foto (Gloeden?)
2426 Herakles Farnese (Neapel)Plastik
2427 Mann mit herkulischen Formen, Foto
2428 Venus v.Medici, Florenz,Plastik;Mädchen in verschämter Haltung, Foto
2429 Die Grazien von Siena,Plastik
243o Drei javan. Mädchen, F.
2431 Die Nacht von Michelangelo, Florenz
2432 4ojährige Frau in gl. Stellung, F.
2433 Der Tag von Michelangelo, Florenz
2434 Mann in gleicher Stellung, F.
2435 Figur von Michelangelo
2436 Alter Mann in gl.Stellung, F.
2437 Nymphen und Silen von Eberlein
2438 Modelle d rechten Nymphe, v Eberlein gestellt, F.

2439 Die Morgenröte von Michelangelo (Florenz)
2440 Mädchen in ähnlicher Stellung, F.
2441 Sehnsucht von Jerman (Plastik)
2442 Das dazu benutzte Modell vom Künstler gestellt, Foto
2443 Badendes Mädchen von Klinger, Plastik
2444 Klingers Modell in gleicher Stellung, Foto
2445 Tänzerin von Falguière, Plastik
2446 Nackte Figur mit Schnürtaille
2447 Venus v. Cranach, Frankfurt
2448 Modell mit Schnürtaille und lässiger Haltung
2449 Erschaffung Adams, Michelangelo, Sixtina, Rom
2450 Jüngerer Mann in der Stellung Adams, F.
2451 Ausgestr.lieg. Gestalt,F., Venus m. Lautenschläger v. Titian
2452 Venus mit Amor und Venus von Urbino, Titian
2453 Rubens, Christus am Kreuz, Gekreuzigter, F.
2454 Ingre, Die Quelle, 15 jähr. Mädchen, F.
2455 Die Wahrheit von Lefèbvre, Gemälde
2456 2ojähr. Pariserin, F.
2457 Gemälde und Foto eines weibl. Aktes
2458 Das Modell des Bildhauers Alma Tadema, Gemälde
2459 Trübner, Titanenkampf, Gemälde
2460 Modelle zum Titanenkampf von Trübner gestellt, F.

Raimund Stillfried von Rathenitz (1839 - 1911)
2461 - Reisefotografien und Aquarelle als Kolorierungsvorlagen von
2499 Raimund Stillfried von Rathenitz zw. 1871 - 1883 aus Tokio/
Yokohama

August Sander, Menschen des 2o. Jh.s. Portraitphotographien 1892 - 1952, München 198o

25oo Bauer, Westserwald 1913
25o1 Bäuerin, Westerwald 1914
25o2 Bauernpaar, Westerwald 1912
25o3 Bäuerin, Westerwald 1913
25o4 Bauernwitwe, Westerwald 1912
25o5 Bauer, Westerwald 191o
25o6 Jungbauern, Westerwald ca 1914
25o7 Jungbauern, Westerwald ca 1912
25o8 Bauernmädchen, ca 1928
25o9 Bäuerliches Brautpaar, ca 1914
251o Konfirmandin, ca 1911
2511 Bäuerliches Geschwisterpaar, 1927/28
2512 Bauernmädchen, Westerwald ca 193o-31
2513 Wanderer, Siegerland, 1892
2514 Bauern beim Kartenspiel, ca 1919
2515 Bauern mit Pferden, ca 193o
2516 Mittagspause im Hauberg, Westerwald, 193o
2517 Bauernfamilie, 1913
2518 Bauernfamilie, Hunsrück, 1919
2519 Bauernfamilie, ca 1913
252o Bauernfamilie, ca 1914
2521 Bauernfamilie, Eifel, ca 1931/32
2522 Bauernkinder, Westerwald, ca 1913
2523 Großmutter und Enkel, ca 1914
2524 Mutter und Sohn, ca 1919
2525 Mutter mit ihren Kindern, ca 192o
2526 Bauernkinder, 1927
2527 Bauernkind, ca 1927
2528 Bäuerliche Braut, 1921/22
2529 Kleinstadtehepaar, Eifel, ca 1926/27
253o Kleinstadtfamilie, Herdorf, ca 1914
2531 Kleinstädterin, ca 1927/28
2532 Boxer Paul Röderstein und Hein Heese, Köln, ca 1928
2533 Jokey, Wien 193o
2534 Sportflieger Köln, ca 192o
2535 Boxer Hein Domgörgen, ca 1927
2536 Konditormeister, Köln-Lindenthal, ca 1928
2537 ~~Schmied, Westerwald, ca 1912/13~~ Sattlermeister, ca 1932

August Sander, Menschen...
2538 Schmied, Westerwald, ca 1912/13
2539 Metzgergeselle, Westerwald 1905/06
2540 Dachdeckermeister, Nürnberg, ca 1932
2541 Schlossermeister, Köln-Lindenthal, ca 1924
2542 Preisträger eines ländlichen Gesangsvereins, 1927
2543 Bauernpaar, ca 1932
2544 Bauer beim Sähen, 1940
2545 Bäuerin, Eifel, ca 1932
2546 Rheinischer Bauer, 1931/32
2547 Bauer. Eifel 1931/32
2548 Bauer. Westerwald, 1932
2549 Vater und Sohn, Westerwald, 1931
2550 Gutherrenehepaar, Kriel bei Köln, ca 1928
2551 Bauernpaar, Westerwald, ca 1932
2552 Bauernpaar, 1912
2553 Bauer, Westerwald, 1931/32
2554 Bauernknecht, 1951
2555 Bauer, Westerwald, ca 1930/31
2556 Alt-Bäuerin, 1932
2557 Laborant, Lamersdorf/Eifel 1932/33
2558 Der Dadaist Raoul Hausmann, Berlin 1928
2559 Der Maler Gottfried Brockmann, Köln 1924
2560 Kunstgelehrter Dr. Karl With, Köln 1932
2561 Der Dadaist Raoul Hausmann, Berlin 1928
2562

Helmar Lerski, Porträt
2563 Helmar Lerski, Porträt
2564 Helmar Lerski, Porträt Serie
2565 Lerski, Araber und Juden
2566 Porträt
2567 Lerski, Porträt Serie
2568 Lerski, Edith Ornstein, ca 1935
2569 Lerski, Max M. Stern, Psychoanalytiker, ca 1937
2570 Jüdin aus Polen
2571 Lerski, Arbeiter
2572 Lerski, Schriftsteller
2573 Lerski, Kibbuz-Arbeiter
2574 Lerski, Metallarbeiter, o.J.
2575 Lerski, Buchhändler 1928-31
2576 Lerski, Adolph Goldschmidt, Kunsthistoriker, ca 1928

Dias Fotogeschichte

2577 Helmar Lerski, Hermann Reckendorf, Verleger, vor 193o

2579 Lerski, H. Reckendorf, vor 193o

2579 Lerski, Die Schauspielerin von Mendelssohn, vor 193o

258o Lerski, Porträt xxx ca 1929

August Sander, Menschen des 2o. Jahrhunderts, Fortsetzung

2581 Sander, Industrieller, Bon ca 1933

2582 Sander , Großindustrieller, Köln 1928

2583 Sander, Schmied, ca 1925/26

2584 Handlanger, ca 1928

2585 Lakierer, Köln 1932

2586 Kohlenträger, Berlin 1929

2587 Arbeiter in der Spinnerei, Hilden 1924

2588 Arbeiter in einer Eisengießerei, Köln 1934

2589 Straßenarbeiter, Ruhrgebiet, ca 1928/29

259o Revolutionäre, in der Mitte E. Mühsam, Berlin 1928

2591 Arbeiterführer Paul Fröhlich, Soz. Arbeiter Partei, Frankf. ca 1928

2592 Künstlerpaar, Otto Dix und seine Frau, Köln 1928

2593 Witwer mit seinen Söhnen, ca 19o6/7

2594 Anna Sander, Frau des Photographen, Linz/Donau, ca 19o2

2595 Frau eines Malers, verheiratet mit Peter Abelen, Köln ca 1927/28

2596 Rundfunksekretärin, Köln 1931

2597 Stenotypistin in einer Sparkasse, Köln 1928

2598 Corpsstudent aus Nürnberg, Köln ca 1928

2599 Corpsstudenten, ca 1928, Köln

26oo Philosoph, Prof. Max Scheler, ca 1925

26o1 Apotheker, Linz/Donau, 1931

Notar, Köln 1924

26o2 Junger Soldat, Westerwald, ca 1945

26o3 Nationalsozialist, ca 1937/38

26o4 Angehöriger der Leibstandarte Adolf Hitler, Köln 1938

26o5 Großherzog von Hessen-Nassau, Darmstadt, 1928

26o6 Katholischer Geistlicher, Köln 1925/26

26o7 Junglehrer, Westerwald, ca 1927/28

26o8 KPD-Funktionäre, E. Mühsam und ein Genosse, 1928

26o9 Mitbegründer der Soz. Arbeiter Partei, ca 1928

261o Abgeordneter der Deutschen Demokratischen Partei, Köln 1928 ca

2611 Zirkusartistin, Köln 1928

2612 Landstreicher, o.D.

2613 Kölner "Hofmusikanten" 1928

2614 Blinde, Düren, ca 193o/31

2615

2616 DAS ALBUM. Titelblatt mit"japanischem Motiv", A. Schumanns Verlag, Paris und Leipzig 19o2

2617 DAS ALBUM. H. Gerbault, Auf dem Opernball, Zeichn. 19o2

2618 DAS ALBUM. H. Morin, Durch's Schlüsselloch oder Suschens Toilette, Zeichnungen 19o2

2619 DAS ALBUM. Arjalew, Die Mondsüchtige, Fot. 19o2

262o DAS ALBUM. Annoncen, u.a. SATYR - Bibliothek, 19o2

2621 DAS ALBUM. H. Manuel, M^lle^Gillet von der Grossen Oper in Paris, Fot

2622 DAS ALBUM. Annoncen, Aktphotographien, 19o2

2623 DAS ALBUM. Annoncen , Aktphotographien, 19o2

2624 DAS ALBUM. o.T. ("DIWANhalbakt")

2625 Daniel Tixier, Frühling, Gemälde

2626 René Le Bègue, Rückkehr der Schwalben, 19o2, Fot.

2627 Ein Wundér der Natur, Fot. Paul Boyer

2628 D. Enjolras, Die Rose, Gemälde

2629 Reutlinger, Eine Pariser Soubrette, M^lle^Méaly, Fot.,

263o M^lle^de Pibrac, Die Paiva, 19o2, Fot.

2631 Diana, Gemälde 19o2

2632 Manuel, Im Seebade, 19o2

2633 Gérome, Die Kugelspielerin, 19o2

2634 L. Berthault, Vor dem Spiegel, 19o2

2635 Zu unseren Bildern (Kommentar zu beiden vorhergehenden Abb.en s.o)

2636Reutlinger, Hasch-Hasch! Fot.

2637 Dr. Georg Buschan, Die Sitten der Völker, Stuttgart, Berlin, Leipzig, Bd. 1-4 o.D. ca 19oo Titelblatt

2638 Buschan, Samoaschönheiten (An.)

2639 Buschan, aus:Kraemer, Samoa. Zwei Mädchen aus Tutuila

264o Buschan, Aus: Hesse-Wartegg, Samoa, Samoanische Taupu

2641 Buschan, aus:Kraemer, Hawai, Marshallinsulanerin

2642 Buschan, aus:Kraemer, Samoainseln, Religiöse Zeremonie d. Beschneidung auf Fidschi

2643 Buschan, Rev. G. Brown, Melanesische Frauen

2644 Buschan, Lirongfrau

2645 Buschan, C.H. Firmin, Haartracht eines Koramaweibes

2646 Buschan, C.H. Firmin, Mädchen der Mendi

Museum für Ur- und Frühgeschichte zu Berlin, Repros nach Originalen

2647 Samuel Bourne & Shepherd, Himalaya, Indien, ca 1875 ?? Mount Everest. Darjeeling

2648 - " -, Brücke über den Rangnoo,Indien

2649 An., Schleife der Bergeisenbahn, Darjeeling, Indien

265o John Burke,Afghanistan

2651 John Burke, Afghanistan

2652 Gruppe von "Haarmenschen" Bourne & Shepherd

2653 Behaarte Familie, Mandelay, Birma

Dias Fotogeschichte

2654 An., Leichenverbrennung eines Kindes in Indien, 189oer
2655 Arbeitselefanten Bangkok, Siam, Ex. v. A. Baessler 1888
Rangoon, Birma, Exp. A. Baessler 1888
2656 Bourne & Shepherd, Groupe of box makers at pagan, Birma
2657 Bourne & Shepherd, Pagoda at Ava
2658 o.A., o.O,, Gelände mit altertüml. Ruinen und Wasserbassin
2659 Pagode, Pagode, Bourne & Shepherd
2660 Andamanen - mit europäischem Forscher
2661 An., Gouverneur, Kambodscha
2662 An., Familie Siam
2663-70 YVA (Else Simon,1900-1942) Mannequins und Filmkomparsinnen mit Schmucksarten aus der süd- und nordamerikanischen Abteilung des Völkerkundemuseums Berlin, Januar 1933 - für Berliner Illustrirte Zeitung, A.P., dort Titelbild (Variante) in Nr. 6, 12. 2.33
2671 Luftbildaufnahme Berlin Zentrum ca 30er Jahre Berliner Museen, ZA
2672 Fr. Albert Schwartz, Berliner Motiv, 1887 DSB
2673 Waldemar Titzenthaler, Waisenhaus Rummelburg,1902, Märk. Mus.
2674 Max Missmann, Spielwiese in Treptow, 1907, Märk. Mus.
2675 Max Missmann, Potsdamer Platz, 1925, Märk. Museum.
2676 Gebr. Haeckel, Zeppelin auf dem Landplatz in Tegel, 1909, Märk. M.
2677 Heinrich Zille, Jahrmarkszelte von hinten, 1890 .1910, Flügge
2678 Heinrich Zille, Sandlandschaft vor Berlin, 1890-1910, Flügge
2679 Ahrens (?) Spree mit Kurfürstenbrücke
2680 Horst P. Horst(1906 -) Porträt Monographie Horst P. Horst
2681 Horst, Porträt
2682 Horst, Modeaufnahme
2683 Horst, d.o.
2684 Horst,d,o, Madame Lucien Lelong
2685 Horstim Abendkleid,
2686 Horst,Lady Ady
2687 HorstModeaufnahme
2688 Horst, Nachtkabarett auf dem Montmartre
2689 Horst,Kameraden
2690 Horst, Auf der Sprungbrücke
2691 Horst, männl. Brustbild, Akt
2692 Horst, männl. Akt
2693 Horst, Brigitte Helm in "Atlantis"
2694 Horst,Lady Ady
2695 Horst, Der Dichter Jean Cocteau
2696 Horst, Der Bildhauer Antoine Bourdelle
2697 Edward Steichen, Selbstbildnis o.D. (20er-30er)
2698 Edward Steichen, Rodin, ca 1900

Karl Blossfeld (1865-1932) Urformen der Kunst, 1928 , Fortsetzung
2699 Delphium. Rittersporn. Teil eines trockenen Blattes 6fach
2700 Saxifraga Willkommniana. Steinbrech. Blattrosette 8 fach
2701 Adiantum pedatum. Haarfarn. Junge gerollte Blätter, 8 fach
2702 Forsythia saspensa. Junger Sproß der Forsitie in 1of Vergr.
2703 Taraxacum officinale. Löwenzahn, Kuhblume , 8 f
2704 Acer furfinerve.Ahorn. Sprossen 1of
2705 Dipsacus laciniatus. Schlitzblättrige Karde. Weberdistel, 4f
2706 Impatiens glanduligera. Balsamine, Springkraut, Nat. Größe

George Hendrik Breitner (1857 - 1923) Gemälde. Zeichnungen, Fotografien, Bonn 1977 Kat. DSB 6 - 31 SA 1772 - 83
2707 Breitner, Das Modell Geesje Kwak im roten Kimono, Foto
2708 Breitner,Mädchen im rotem Kimono, ca 1893, Gemälde
2709 Breitner, Tanzende Dienstmädchen am Hertjesdag
2710 Breitner, Hafenpartie beim Zentralbahnhof
2711 Breitner, Kirmes auf dem Haarlemmerplein
2712 Breitner, Raadhuisstraat mit Blick zur Herengracht, 1895-96
2713 Breitner, Leidseplein
2714 Breitner, Das Modell für das Gemälde "Die Arbeiterin"
2715 Breitner, Arbeiter auf der Baustelle Van Diemenstraat,1897
2716 Breitner, Fünf Bauarbeiter auf der Baustelle d.o., 1897
2717 Breitner, Korte Prinsengracht
2718 Breitner, Cruquisweg
2719 Breitner,Elandsgracht ?
2720 Breitner, Häuserwände (Abbruch)
2721 Breitner,- Porträt von Willem Witsen, Foto

Katalog Das Lichtbildnis, Bonn HRsg, Klaus Honnef
2722 Dr. Homas John Barnardo, Sarah Burge, 5.1.1883
2723 Dr. Thomas John Barnardo, Thomas Bayes, um 1880
2724 Etienne Carjat, Charles Baudelaire, 1859
2725 George Platt Lynes, Max Ernst, ca 1840
2726 Edward Steichen, August Rodin, 1902
2727 Nadar, Charles Garnier, ca 1880
2728 Hugo Erfurth, Käthe Kollwitz, 1935
2729 George Platt Lynes, Elinor Flynn-Cecil Beaton als E.F., ca 1930
2730 Cecil Beaton, Gertrude Stein, 1936
2731 Cecil Baton , Edith Sitwell, 1926
2732 Ralph Gibson

2733 Ralph Gibson
2734 Ralph Gibson
2735 Bill Brandt, Akt, März 1952
2736 Nathan Lerner, Gesicht mit Vergrößerungsglas, 194o
2737 Walter Peterhans, o.T. ca 193o, Porträt
2738 Erwin Blumenfeld, Cecil Beaton, 1936/37
2739 Porträt, Liegende
274o Erwin Blumenfeld, Projektion einer Linie auf einem Gesicht, 1949
2741 Benjamin Stone, PC George Watson und P.C. Henry Harvey, 19o7
2742 John Gutman, Day Dreams, 1939
2743 Benjamin Stone, Newick und Plummer, 19o1
2744 Edward Steichen, Pierpont Morgan, 19o3
2745 Rudolf Dührkoop, Bürgermeister Dr. Buchard, 19o6
2746 Hermann Biow, Jacob Venedy, Abgenordneter der Frankfurter Nationalversammlung, 1848
2747 Roger Fenton, General Sir David de Lacy Edvans, 1855
2748 Hermann Biow, Optiker Andreas Krüss u.s. Familie, Dag. 1845
2749 Roger Fenton, General Sir Jarry Jones, 1855
275o Antoine - Samuel Adam - Salomon, Legouve, ca 188o (Portr.)
2751 Lazergue, Dallemagne: L. Matout, 186o
2752 Hippolyte Lazergue, J.-F.-M. Dallemagne, A.L. Barye, ca 186o
2753 Alexander Gardner, General Parker, ca 1864
2754 Mathew Brady, General A.E. Burnside, ca 1863
2755 Mathew Brady, Abraham Lincoln, 27.2.186o
2756 Alexander Gardner, General Heintzelmann, ca 1864
Repros nach Originalen
2757 Carl Ferdinand Stelzner (18o4-94), Doppelbildnis, o.D. Dag. REPRO
2759 Trottier, Paris, Herrenbildnis, Dag. REPRO
2758 Stelzner, Rückseite einer Daguerreotypie R
276o Trottier, Rückseite ei. Dag. R
2761 An., Mädchenbildnis, Dag., Privatcoll, Fr.M R
2762 An., Damenbildnis, Dag., privcoll, Fr.M R
2763 An.Büste (Plastik) Dag, Privcoll FR. M R
2764 An., Familienbildnis, Dag, Priv coll FR M R
2765 An., Stereo Akt Dag, franz. 1855, Agfa-Foto-Historama R
2766 Stereo.Akt Dag, franz ca 1855, Agfa-Foto-Historama R
2767 An., amerikan. Dag., 1/4 Plate, Coll. Siegert, München, R
2768 An., Grand Harbons, Malta, Blick auf Vittoriosa, ca 188o R
2769 Baldus, Paris, 186oer Coll S Pastor Köln R
277o Baldus, Paris, 186oer Coll. S. Pastor, Köln R
2771 An., Belgien, Hundekarren ca 1885 13 x 18 coll Hca Göttingen R
2772 Renger-Patzsch, Bad Harzburg, ca 193o R
2773 George Washington Wilson, Wells Cathedral, ca 1885, Vorgänger von A sea of steps v Frederick H. Evans

2774 Frith, Araber R
2775 Giorgio Sommer, Napoli: Luzern, Milchmann R
2776 Harry Burton, Tutantchammn-Tomb Photographs, ca 1922-24
2777 Harry Burton, Tutantchammn ... Unibib. Heidelberg R
2778 Binz, Im Familiebad, R
2779 NPG Postkarte, Regen am Meer, 1905 Coll hca , Göttingen R
2780 Paul Martin, Eng., Schwimmer, 1905 R
2781 Schwimmerin im Atlier, Libr. of Congress, Washington DC R
2782 Louis Boutan, 1. Unterwasserschwimmer, Frankf., ca 1889 Magnesiumslicht R
2783 Kertesz, Schwimmer, 1917 R
2784 Munkacsi swimming + photographing R
2785 Martin Munkacsi, Liberia oder Tanganikasee, ca 1932 R
2786 An., Norderney, ca 1930 coll hca, Göttingen R
2787 Edward Weston, Floating Nude, ca 1935 R
2788 Cartier - Bresson, o.T., Akt, schwimmend, ca 1932 R
2789 Harry Callahan, Eleanor, 1949 R
2790 Walter Gropius, swimming, ca 1960 R
2791 Harry Callahan, Lake Michigan ?, ca 1968 R
2792 David Hockney, John St. Clair swimming, ca 1968 R
2793 Ralph Gibson, ca 1968 (Schwimmende) R
2794 AP, Mao swimming th yangtse, ca 1970 R
2795 Arne Raffael Minkkinen, ca 1974, Bern (Schwimmer) R
2796 Etienne Jules Marey, Möwenflug, 1887
2797 Marey, Sprung der Fußgelenke auf der Stelle, ca 1886
2798 Marey, Sprung über ein Hindernis, 1884
2799 Marey, Gang eines Elefanten mit Markierungen, 1886/87
2800 Marey, Prallender Ball, 1886
2801 Marey, Vertikaler Fall eines weißen Balls, 1884, Neapel
2802 Marey, Trottendes Pferd, 1886
2803 Marey, Galoppierendes Pferd, 1886
2804 Marey, Gang eines nackten Kindes, nach 1886
2805 Marey, Möwe im Flug, Vergrößerung eines Moment-Teilbildes, 1886
2806 Marey, Studie über den Gang, etwa 1886
2807 Marey, Mann in Weiß vor dem ersten schwarzen Fond, 1882
2808 Marey, "Gelenkbewegungen", Drehung des Kopfes, 1884
2809 Marey, Luftbewegungen (Rauchschwaden, Kugel), 1900
2810 Marey, Mann im Lauf, gegen 1891
2811 Marey, Wellenschlägen, sichtbar gemacht, 1892.93
aus: Etienne Jules Marey, Paris (Photo-Poche)

Agfa-Foto-Historama,
Bodo v. Dewitz, Reinhard Matz (Hrg), Silber und Salz,
Köln 1989, Katalog

2812 Hermann Biow, Susanna Hahn mit 7 ihrer 11 Kinder, Hamburg 1843 Dag.
2813 Carl Ferdinand Stelzner, Die Tänzerin Maria Taglioni, 1804-84, Hamburg 1845, Dag.
2814 Carl F. Stelzner, 2 Kinder Stelzners, 1856, Dag., kol (Alfred und Bruno)
2815 C.F. Stelzner, Stelzners 2 Frau, 1852 , Anna Henriette
2816 Stelzner, Familienporträt der Familie Mesecke, Stade ca 1847
1817 Stelzner, Mutter Albers, die Gemüsefrau der Familie, ca 1845, Dag.
2818 Hermann Biow, Ein Vater mit s. 6 Söhnen, Hamburg, ca 1845, Dag.
2819 H. Biow, Susanna Hahn mit 7 ihrer 11 Kinder, 1843 Dag.
2820 Stelzner, Maria Taglioni, ca 1845 Dag.
2821 Stelzner, Die Miniaturmalerin Caroline Stelzner, ca 1843 Dag.
2822 Porträt Stelzners, Gemälde , Selbstbildnis, Hamburg 1833
2823 Akademien, Stereodaguerreotypien, 5oer
2824 d.o. um 1855 o.O
2825 pornograph. Darstellungen, 5oer Jahre
2826 Akademien, Stereodag. um 1855
2827 Damenbildnisse, Stereodag. um 1855
2828 Akademien, Stereodag. um 1855 o,O.
2829 pornograph. Darstellungen, 5oer Jahre
2830 Akademien, 5oer Jahre
2831 Hermann Biow, Christian Daniel Rauch, Berlin 1847
2832 Hermann Biow, Porträt Peter von Cornelius, Berlin 1847
2833 Hermann Biow, Friedrich Wilhelm IV, König v. Preußen Bln 1847
2834 Hermann Biow, Jacob Venedy, Abgeordneter v. Hamburg in der Frankfurter Nationalver
2835 Biow, Dr. jur Paul Hermann, Abgeordneter von Bautzen 1848
2836 Herm.Biow Alexander von Humboldt Berlin 1847
2837 Franz Hanfstaengl, Ida Birch-Pfeiffer, Weltreisende, 1 850er
2838 Hanfstaengl, Philipp Martius, Naturforscher, 1856
2839 Hanfstaengl, König MaxII von Bayern, 1856
2840 Hanfstaengl, Clara Schumann, 1856
2841 Hanfstaengl, Franz Liszt, 1856
2842 Hanfstaengl, Leo von Klenze, 1856
2843 Franz Hanfstaengl, ~~Prinzessin~~ Königin Marie von Bayern, 1856
2844 Hanfstaengl, Dr. Gustav Scheve, Arzt u Phrenologe, 1856
2845 Hanfstaengl, Selbstporträt, um 1853
2846 Alois Löcherer, Herr Christian , München um 1850, Salzpapier
2847 A. Löcherer, Bildnis eines Ehepaares, um 1852, München, Salzp.

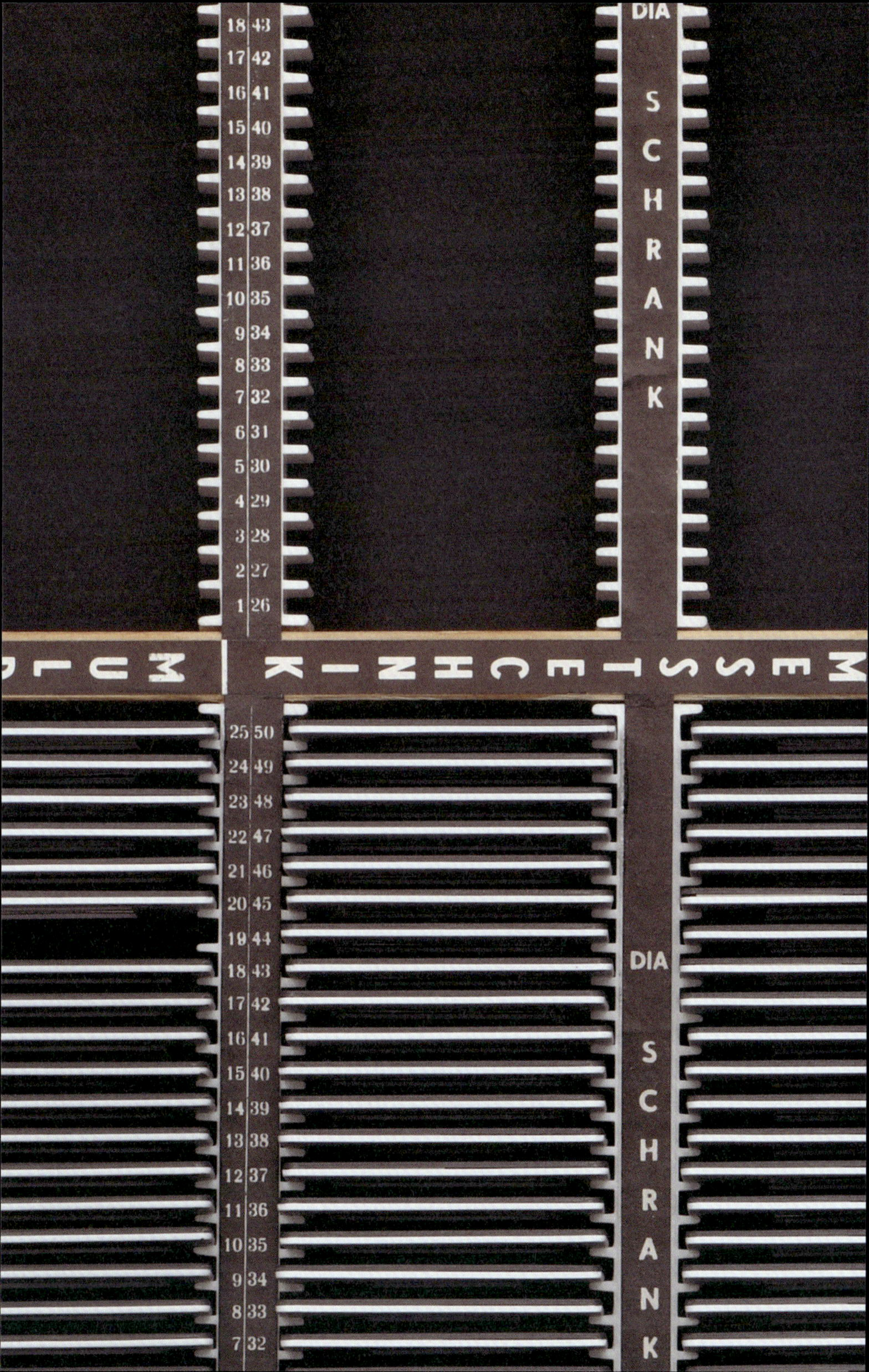

DIA SCHRANK
DIA SCHRANK

2848 A. Löcherer, Porträt Carl Rahl 1848.5o
2849 A. Löcherer, Eduard Schleich der Aältere, 185o
285o A. Löcherer, Wilhelm von Kaulbach, München ca 185o
2851 A. Löcherer, Justus von Liebig,
2852 A. Löcherer, Kopf der 1844 gegossenen Bavaria, 1848-5o
2853 A. Löcherer, Bearbeitung des Bruststückes der Bavaria, 1848-5o
2854 A. Löcherer, Kopf der Bavaria, 1848-5o
2855 A. Löcherer, Transport der Bavaria, München, 7.8.185o
2856 A. Löcherer, Guß eines Löwen der Siegesthor-Quadriga, 1848-5o
2857 A. Löcherer, Joseph Albert, München , vor 185o
2858 Hermann Krone, Drei Pifferari, Dresden ca 1855 Salzpap.
2859 Hermann Krone, Drei Schauspieler als Radomonth, Ferragu und Zagripont beim Schnorrfest in Dresden, 1852
286o H. Krone, Lehrtafel Nr. 2 zum Kalotypischen Negativ Aufnahmen Dresden 1852
2861 H. Krone, Lehrtafel Nr. 83 zum Verfahren von Albuminvergr. Dresden 1853 - 78
2862 H. Krone, Lehrtafel Nr. 9 mit 25 Photographien v.d. Sächs. Schweiz, 1858
2863 H. Krone, Selbstporträt des Photographen neben seinen Objektiven, Dresden 1858
2864 H. Krone, Werbeplakat mit aufgeklebten Photographien Dresden um 186o
2865 H. Krone, "Beim Astrologen" - Atelierinszenierung mit Herrn Rehahn, einem Dresdner Original, Dresden um 1855
2866 H. Krone, Lehrtafel Nr. 37 mit 87 Photographien zur Einführung des Visitkartenformats, Dresden 1859
2867 H. Krone, Lehrtafel Nr. 29 zur Trockenmethode, Dresden 1855
2868 H. Krone, Lehrtafel Nr. 13 zum Kollodiumverfahren, Dresden 53.
2869 H. Krone, Lehrtafel Nr. 86 zur Kolorierung, Dresden 1857
287o H. Krone, Drei Schauspieler als Gernot, Gunther und Giselher beim Schnorrfest in Dresden 1862
2871 Atlier, Das Ehepaar Krone, Dresden um 1855

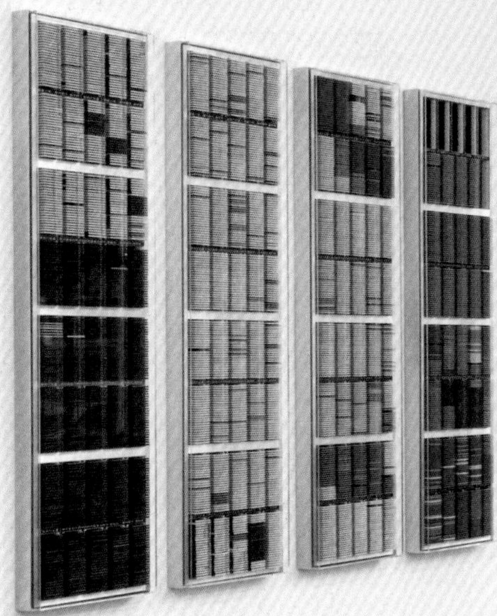

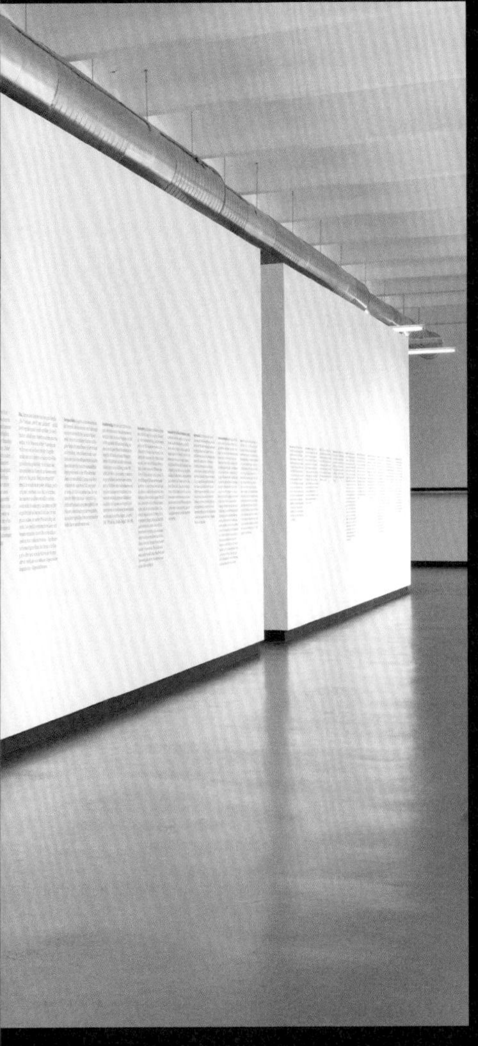

Philipp Goldbach, Steffen Siegel, *Lossless Compression (Diathek Fotografiegeschichte Andreas Krase)*, 3835 small format slides in four frames from original slide cabinets of VEB Foto und Feinmesstechnik Mulda (120 × 33.5 × 7.5 cm each), wall texts, 2024

KONTEXT – a series by DISTANZ.

Acknowledgments

Matthias Kliefoth and Rebecca Wilton thank Philipp Goldbach, Andreas Krase and Steffen Siegel.

Imprint

Editors
Matthias Kliefoth, Rebecca Wilton

Design
Mali Wychodil

Design Concept KONTEXT
Manuel Tayarani

Copy Editing
Rebecca Wilton

Image Editing
max-color, Berlin

Production
Marcus Sabsch

Printing and Binding
Druckhaus Sportflieger, Berlin

ISBN 978-3-95476-751-9

Printed in Germany

Published by
DISTANZ Verlag
www.distanz.de